# ELIZABETH I

WORLD LEADERS   PAST AND PRESENT

# ELIZABETH I

Catherine Bush

*Burke Publishing Company Limited*
*LONDON ∗ TORONTO ∗ NEW YORK*

First published in the United States of America 1985
© 1985 by Chelsea House Publishers,
a division of Chelsea House Communications, Inc.
Introduction © 1985 by Arthur M. Schlesinger, Jr.
New material included in this edition.
© Burke Publishing Company Limited 1988.

ACKNOWLEDGEMENTS
The Author and Publishers are grateful to the Bettmann Archive, the
Mansell Collection and the New York Public Library for their permission to
reproduce copyright illustrations in this book.

**CIP data**
Bush, Catherine
    Elizabeth I.
    1. England. Elizabeth I, Queen of England –
    Biographies
    I. Title
    942.05'5'0924

    ISBN 0 222 01327 3 Hardbound
    ISBN 0 222 01328 1 Paperback

Burke Publishing Company Limited
Pegasus House, 116–120 Golden Lane, London EC1Y 0TL, England
Printed in England by Purnell Book Production Limited.

# CONTENTS

# WORLD LEADERS  PAST AND PRESENT

KONRAD ADENAUER
ALEXANDER THE GREAT
MARK ANTONY
KING ARTHUR
KEMAL ATATÜRK
CLEMENT ATTLEE
MENACHEM BEGIN
DAVID BEN GURION
BISMARCK
LÉON BLUM
SÍMON BOLÍVAR
CESARE BORGIA
WILLY BRANDT
LEONID BREZHNEV
JULIUS CEASAR
CALVIN
FIDEL CASTRO
CATHERINE THE GREAT
CHARLEMAGNE
CHIÀNG KAI-SHEK
CHOU EN-LAI
WINSTON CHURCHILL
CLEMENCEAU
CLEOPATRA
CORTES
CROMWELL
DANTON
CHARLES DE GAULLE
DE VALERA
DISRAELI
DWIGHT D. EISENHOWER
ELEANOR OF AQUITAINE
QUEEN ELIZABETH I

FERDINAND AND ISABELLA
FRANCO
FREDERICK THE GREAT
INDIRA GANDHI
MOHANDAS K. GANDHI
GARIBALDI
GENGHIS KHAN
GLADSTONE
DAG HAMMARSKJÖLD
HENRY VIII
HENRY OF NAVARRE
HINDENBURG
ADOLF HITLER
HO CHI MINH
KING HUSSEIN
IVAN THE TERRIBLE
ANDREW JACKSON
THOMAS JEFFERSON
JOAN OF ARC
POPE JOHN XXIII
LYNDON JOHNSON
BENITO JUÁREZ
JOHN F. KENNEDY
JOMO KENYATTA
AYATOLLAH KHOMEINI
NIKITA KHRUSHCHEV
MARTIN LUTHER KING
HENRY KISSINGER
VLADIMIR LENIN
ABRAHAM LINCOLN
LLOYD GEORGE
LOUIS XIV
MARTIN LUTHER
JUDAS MACCABEUS

MAO TSE TUNG
MARY, QUEEN OF SCOTS
GOLDA MEIR
METTERNICH
BENITO MUSSOLINI
NAPOLEON
JAMAL NASSER
JAWALHARLAL NEHRU
NERO
NICHOLAS II
RICHARD NIXON
KWAME NKRUMAH
PERICLES
JUAN PERÓN
MUAMMAR QADDAFI
ROBESPIERRE
ELEANOR ROOSEVELT
FRANKLIN D. ROOSEVELT
THEODORE ROOSEVELT
ANWAR SADAT
SUN YAT-SEN
JOSEPH STALIN
TAMERLANE
MARGARET THATCHER
IOSIF TITO
LEON TROTSKY
PIERRE TRUDEAU
HARRY S. TRUMAN
QUEEN VICTORIA
GEORGE WASHINGTON
CHAIM WEIZMANN
WOODROW WILSON
XERXES

LEADERSHIP, it may be said, is really what makes the world go round. Love no doubt smooths the passage; but love is a private transaction between consenting adults. Leadership is a public transaction with history. The idea of leadership affirms the capacity of individuals to move, inspire and mobilize masses of people so that they act together in pursuit of an end. Sometimes leadership serves good purposes, sometimes bad; but whether the end is benign or evil, great leaders are those men and women who leave their personal stamp on history.

Now, the very concept of leadership implies the proposition that individuals can make a difference. This proposition has never been universally accepted. From classical times to the present day, eminent thinkers have regarded individuals as no more than the agents and pawns of larger forces, whether the gods and goddesses of the ancient world or, in the modern era, race, class, nation, the dialectic, the will of the people, the spirit of the times, history itself. Against such forces, the individual dwindles into insignificance.

So contends the thesis of historical determinism. Tolstoy's great novel *War and Peace* offers a famous statement of the case. Why, Tolstoy asked, did millions of men in the Napoleonic wars, denying their human feelings and their common sense, move back and forth across Europe slaughtering their fellows? "The war," Tolstoy answered, "was bound to happen simply because it was bound to happen." All prior history predetermined it. As for leaders, they, Tolstoy said, "are but the labels that serve to give a name to an end and, like labels, they have the least possible connection with the event." The greater the leader, "the more conspicuous the inevitability and the predestination of every act he commits." The leader, said Tolstoy, is "the slave of history".

Determinism takes many forms. Marxism is the determinism of class, Nazism the determinism of race. But the idea of men and women as the slaves of history runs athwart the deepest human instincts. Rigid determinism abolishes the idea of human freedom—the assumption of free choice that underlies every move we make, every word we speak, every thought we think. It abolishes the idea of human responsibility, since it is manifestly unfair to reward or punish people for actions that are by definition beyond their control. No one can live consistently by any deterministic creed. The Marxist states prove this themselves by their extreme susceptibility to the cult of leadership.

More than that, history refutes the idea that individuals make no difference. In December 1931 a British politician crossing Park Avenue in New York City between 76th and 77th Streets around ten-thirty at night looked in the wrong direction and was knocked down by a speeding car—a moment, he later recalled, of a man aghast, a world aglare: "I do not understand why I was not broken like an eggshell or squashed like a gooseberry." Fourteen months later an American politician, sitting in an open car in Miami, Florida, was fired on by an assassin; the man beside him was hit. Those who believe that individuals make no difference to history might well ponder whether the next two decades would have been the same, had Mario Contasini's car killed Winston Churchill in 1931 and had Giuseppe Zangara's bullet killed Franklin Roosevelt in 1933. Suppose, in addition, that Adolf Hitler had been killed in the street fighting during the Munich *Putsch* of 1923 and that Lenin had died of typhus during the First World War. What would the 20th century be like now?

For better or for worse, individuals do make a difference. "The notion that a people can run itself and its affairs anonymously," wrote the philosopher William James, "is now well known to be the silliest of absurdities. Mankind does nothing save through initiatives on the part of inventors, great or small, and imitation by the rest of us—these are the sole factors in human progress. Individuals of genius show the way, and set the patterns, which common people then adopt and follow."

Leadership, James suggests, means leadership in thought as well as in action. In the long run, leaders in thought may well make the greater difference to the world. But, as Woodrow Wilson once said, "Those only are leaders of men, in the general eye, who lead in action . . . It is at their hands that new thought gets its translation into the crude language of deeds." Leaders in thought often invent in solitude and obscurity, leaving to later generations the tasks of imitation. Leaders in action—the leaders portrayed in this series—have to be effective in their own time.

And they cannot be effective by themselves. They must act in response to the rhythms of their age. Their genius must be adapted, in a phrase of William James's, "to the receptivities of the moment". Leaders are useless without followers. "There goes the mob," said the French politician hearing a clamour in the streets. "I am their leader. I must follow them." Great leaders turn the inchoate emotions of the mob to purposes of their own. They seize on the opportunities of their time, the hopes, fears, frustrations, crises, potentialities. They succeed when events have prepared the way for them, when the community is waiting to be aroused, when they can provide the clarifying and organizing ideas. Leadership ignites the circuit between the individual and the mass and thereby alters history. It may alter history for better or for worse. Leaders have been responsible for the most extravagant follies and most monstrous crimes that have beset suffering humanity. They have also been vital in such gains as humanity has made in individual freedom, religious and racial tolerance, social justice and respect for human rights.

There is no sure way to tell in advance who is going to lead for good and who for evil. But a glance at the gallery of men and women in *World Leaders—Past and Present* suggests some useful tests.

One test is this: do leaders lead by force or by persuasion? By command or by consent? Through most of history leadership was exercised by the divine right of authority. The duty of followers was to defer and to obey. *"Their's not to reason why,/Their's but to do and die."* On occasion, as with the so-called "enlightened despots" of the 18th century in Europe, absolutist leadership was animated by humane purposes. More often, absolutism nourished the passion for domination, land, gold and conquest and resulted in tyranny.

The great revolution of modern times has been the revolution of equality. The idea that all people should be equal in their legal condition has undermined the old structures of authority, hierarchy and deference. The revolution of equality has had two contrary effects on the nature of leadership. For equality, as Alexis de Tocqueville pointed out in his great study *Democracy in America,* might mean equality in servitude as well as equality in freedom.

"I know of only two methods of establishing equality in the political world," Tocqueville wrote. "Rights must be given to every citizen, or none at all to anyone . . . save one, who is the master of all." There was no middle ground "between the sovereignty of all and the absolute power of one man". In his astonishing prediction of 20th-century totalitarian dictatorship, Tocqueville explained how the revolution of equality could lead to the *Führerprinzip* and more terrible absolutism than the world had ever known.

But when rights are given to every citizen and the sovereignty of all is established, the problem of leadership takes a new form, becomes more exacting than ever before. It is easy to issue commands and enforce them by the rope and the stake, the concentration camp and the *gulag.* It is much harder to use argument and achievement to overcome opposition and win consent. The Founding Fathers of the United States understood the difficulty. They believed that history had given them the opportunity to decide, as Alexander Hamilton wrote in the first Federalist Paper, whether men are indeed capable of basing government on "reflection and choice, or whether they are forever destined to depend . . . on accident and force."

Government by reflection and choice called for a new style of leadership and a new quality of followership. It required leaders to be responsive to popular concerns, and it required followers to be active and informed participants in the process. Democracy does not eliminate emotion from politics; sometimes it fosters demagogy; but it is confident that, as the greatest of democratic leaders put it, you cannot fool all of the people all of the time. It measures leadership by results and retires those who overreach or falter or fail.

It is true that in the long run despots are measured by results too. But they can postpone the day of judgement, sometimes indefinitely, and in the meantime they can do infinite harm. It is also true that democracy is no guarantee of virtue and intelligence in government, for the voice of the people is not necessarily the voice of God. But democracy, by assuring the rights of opposition, offers built-in resistance to the evils inherent in absolutism. As the theologian Reinhold Niebuhr summed it up, "Man's capacity for justice makes democracy possible, but man's inclination to injustice makes democracy necessary."

A second test for leadership is the end for which power is sought. When leaders have as their goal the supremacy of a master race or the promotion of totalitarian revolution or the acquisition and exploitation of colonies or the protection of greed and privilege or the preservation of personal power, it is likely that their leadership will do little to advance the cause of humanity. When their goal is the abolition of slavery, the liberation of women, the enlargement of opportunity for the poor and powerless, the extension of equal rights to racial minorities, the defence of the freedoms of expression and opposition, it is likely that their leadership will increase the sum of human liberty and welfare.

Leaders have done great harm to the world. They have also conferred great benefits. You will find both sorts in this series. Even "good" leaders must be regarded with a certain wariness. Leaders are not demigods; they put on their trousers one leg after another just like ordinary mortals. No leader is infallible, and every leader needs to be reminded of this at regular intervals. Irreverence irritates leaders but is their salvation. Unquestioning submission corrupts leaders and demeans followers. Making a cult of a leader is always a mistake. Fortunately hero worship generates its own antidote. "Every hero," said Emerson, "becomes a bore at last."

The signal benefit the great leaders confer is to embolden the rest of us to live according to our own best selves, to be active, insistent, and resolute in affirming our own sense of things. For great leaders attest to the reality of human freedom against the supposed inevitabilities of history. And they attest to the wisdom and power that may lie within the most unlikely of us, which is why Abraham Lincoln remains the supreme example of great leadership. A great leader, said Emerson, exhibits new possibilities to all humanity. "We feed on genius . . . Great men exist that there may be greater men."

Great leaders, in short, justify themselves by emancipating and empowering their followers. So humanity struggles to master its destiny, remembering with Alexis de Tocqueville: "It is true that around every man a fatal circle is traced beyond which he cannot pass; but within the wide verge of that circle he is powerful and free; as it is with man, so with communities."

ARTHUR M. SCHLESINGER JR.
*New York*

# 1

# A Daughter Instead

Staring disconsolately at the grey waters of the Thames River, and quite oblivious of the beauty of the English countryside, Anne Boleyn, queen of England, rode in her royal barge to imprisonment in the tower. In this grim fortress, for more than 400 years, traitors to the crown had been detained and put to death at the monarch's pleasure.

According to an old English song, the month of May was supposedly a merry one, a time for rejoicing at the coming of spring. But May 2, 1536, was a fateful date for this hapless queen. Her journey that day was to be the last she would ever make. Anne knew that having once entered London's mighty citadel she would never leave alive. On the orders of her husband, King Henry VIII, she was to be executed for treason.

As head of church and state, Henry commanded the absolute obedience of all his subjects, gentlemen and commoners alike. As the king wished, so it was done. His will was incontestable. His wives and his warriors, his statesmen and servants—all were at his mercy.

When the splendid vessel, shrouded in silence

Catherine of Aragon, Henry VIII's first wife, was the daughter of Ferdinand and Isabella of Spain, the sovereigns who supported Christopher Columbus's 1492 voyage to the New World. Catherine lived for three years after Henry ended their marriage in 1533, enduring her undeserved misfortune with courage and understanding.

Catherine of Aragon (1485–1536) begs her impassive husband, Henry VIII of England (1491–1547), not to divorce her. Presiding over the 1529 church hearing is Thomas Wolsey (1475–1530), the powerful cardinal who lost favour with Henry when he failed to persuade Pope Clement VII (1478–1534) to give his consent to the king's request for a divorce.

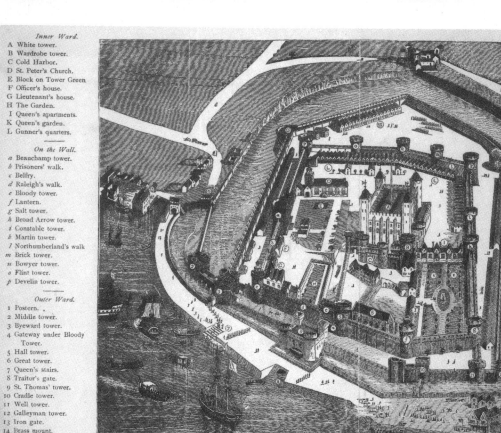

VIEW OF HER MAJESTY'S TOWER IN THE REIGN OF ELIZABETH.

**Built around William the Conqueror's 11th-century White Tower (centre, with flagpole), the Tower of London was used as a royal conference site for many years and remains the repository for the Crown Jewels. The Tower has also served as a prison and place of execution for political offenders and spies.**

and sadness, drew level with Henry's riverside palace, Anne made one last desperate attempt to regain the compassion of the man whose love and affection she had thought would never end following their first meeting in 1522. Holding up Elizabeth, the daughter she had borne him in 1533, Anne begged the king for mercy—at least for Elizabeth's sake. But King Henry would not even turn to look at his wife and child.

Yet it had been in order to legitimize his marriage to Anne (the sister of one of his many previous mistresses) that Henry VIII of England had taken an unprecedented step only two years earlier. Provoking a cataclysmic reaction all across Europe, he had broken away from the Catholic Church in March 1534. But there was an even deeper reason for his drastic step: Henry wanted a son to succeed him. His rejection of Catholicism was the culmination of a running battle with the papal authorities in which he had been engaged since 1527.

Henry, like most people in the 16th century, believed that it was unnatural for a woman to rule over men. Though a royal daughter could inherit the throne, she was not expected actually to hold power. Indeed, women were thought to be weaker than men in all respects and completely incapable of taking charge of affairs of state.

While all monarchs were obliged to marry in order to provide an heir to the throne, when a queen wed her power passed to her husband. This tradition could cause great complications regarding national sovereignty when the ruling houses of two countries were involved. Henry realized that if he were to be succeeded by a daughter and she then married a European prince, England stood to lose its independence and become little more than a foreign possession. Fathering a male heir was to become Henry's greatest purpose in life, and he was determined to succeed whatever the cost.

Henry's first wife, Catherine of Aragon (whom he had married in 1509) had been unable to give him the son he wanted. Her first four children had died at birth or during early infancy. The arrival of the fifth, in 1516, quite failed to diminish Henry's preoccupation with insuring male succession. The

**Martin Luther (1483–1546) is known as the "Father of the Reformation". Although his antipapal doctrines made it easier for Henry VIII to break with Rome, the king never accepted Luther's views or considered Protestantism a true and legal faith.**

**Visitors to 16th-century London were awestruck by the capital's size, diversity, and architectural splendour. Many Elizabethans considered London Bridge (centre) one of the wonders of the world.**

Henry VIII's request for a divorce from Catherine of Aragon created a painful dilemma for Pope Clement VII, who desperately wanted Henry's help to prevent the spread of Protestantism in England, but dared not incur the wrath of the Holy Roman emperor, Charles V, Catherine's powerful nephew.

John Calvin (1509–1564) started the religious movement later called Puritanism. Bitterly opposed to Catholicism, the Calvinists—like the Lutherans—downgraded the role of the clergy, believing the Bible to be the only source of God's word and the individual human conscience its only proper interpreter.

child survived, but since it was a girl her father was hardly overjoyed. Henry was a very devout man who loved nothing better than discussions of the intricacies of religious doctrine. He began to believe that four consecutive disastrous births followed by the survival of a mere daughter constituted a sign that God was punishing him for previous misdemeanours. He came to suspect that he should never have married Catherine, who had briefly been his brother Arthur's wife before Arthur's early death— marrying one's brother's wife was forbidden by the current interpretation of the Bible.

Since divorce was not allowed within the Catholic Church, Henry petitioned Pope Clement VII to have his marriage annulled. For reasons political rather than religious, however, 1527 was not a good year in which to ask this particular favour of the pope. Catherine's nephew, the Holy Roman emperor Charles V, had recently crowned his tremendously successful efforts to make himself the most powerful ruler in Europe by savagely sacking Rome and taking the pope prisoner. Pope Clement understandably had no intention of risking his already reduced authority and prestige by angering the man at whose mercy he found himself. Charles considered Henry's divorce petition an insult to his aunt and, therefore, to his own person. He made it quite clear to Clement that giving in to Henry's demands would result in further devastation of Rome by the imperial armies.

Henry soon realized that he would simply have to make his own arrangements. Towards the end of 1532, after much political and religious manoeuvring, Henry secured for Thomas Cranmer, the archbishop of Canterbury and England's leading churchman, many of those powers which had previously rested with the pope. Cranmer promptly annulled Henry's marriage to Catherine of Aragon and the delighted king married Anne Boleyn on January 25, 1533.

During the winter of 1533–34 Henry continued to push new legislation through Parliament, paving the way for a final break with Rome. The confidence he had shown in crowning Anne queen on June 1,

1533, made it clear to all the courts in Christendom that England's king would have his own way in all matters. Finally, early in 1534, Henry declared himself head of the Church of England. It was an extreme act, but at the time there was much opposition to Catholicism. Throughout Europe the Reformation movement was attacking the Catholic Church, criticizing it for its worldly power and corruption.

The widespread dissatisfaction of many ordinary Catholics with the condition of their church at the beginning of the 16th century had found its first major focus for reform in 1519, when a German priest named Martin Luther had publicly denied the supremacy of the pope. Coming hard upon the heels of his previous attack on the papal practice of selling indulgences (whereby sinners were promised freedom from punishment after death for the price of a contribution to the Vatican), Luther's eloquent denial of papal supremacy greatly increased the intellectual credentials of the Reformation. Another leading figure in the revolt against Rome was the French theologian John Calvin, a brilliant writer and teacher who first declared his support for religious reform in 1528 and later founded a theocratic and violently anti-Catholic government in the Swiss city of Geneva, thus making it a focus for the defence of Protestantism.

Indeed, Henry's break with Rome was but one symptom of the religious turmoil then affecting Europe. He had also created a new kind of monarchy. The old, medieval, feudal monarchy, which depended on the support of a powerful nobility, had already been abandoned. Now the king was not only the source of political power, but of spiritual authority as well. In addition, his treasury swelled with the wealth and lands that had formerly belonged to the Catholic abbeys and monasteries. Thus Henry became an absolute monarch, answerable to no one other than God. And yet he knew only too well that there was one thing his supremacy could never guarantee him—a son.

Anne Boleyn was already pregnant when she

Pope Clement VII (left) allied the papacy with England, France, Venice, and Milan to oppose the advance of Charles V (right) in the Italian peninsula. After Charles defeated the League of Cognac and sacked Rome, Clement switched his loyalty and, in 1530, crowned Charles (1500-1558) Holy Roman emperor.

married Henry, and throughout the early months of 1533 the court astrologers had confidently predicted that her child would be a boy. But on September 7 Anne gave birth to a daughter—to her despair and Henry's fury. He had not defied the pope, endangering both his crown and his kingdom, for a girl. Certainly, he thought, all the courts of Europe must be laughing at him.

Although Henry did not attend, his daughter Elizabeth was still given a lavish christening. Londoners celebrated the birth of a royal child with bonfires. After all, in an age when many children died at birth, people were at least thankful that the baby was alive and healthy. And for the present she was "Princess Elizabeth", while her 17-year-old half-sister (Henry's daughter by Catherine of Aragon), who had been declared illegitimate, was called simply "Lady Mary". In fact, in the household that prepared for the birth of Anne Boleyn's child, Mary was treated more like a servant than a daughter of royalty.

The first three years of Elizabeth's life passed without incident. The little princess was far too

Henry VIII is usually portrayed as he is seen in this painting by Hans Holbein (1497–1543): a huge man, famed for his rowdy ways and lusty appetites. When he ascended to the throne in 1509, however, he was handsome, athletic, musically gifted, extremely well-read, and a truly devoted patron of the arts.

Anne Boleyn (1507–1536) dances with Henry VIII (left) in the happy days that preceded their marriage. At first passionately in love with his young queen, Henry grew cold towards her when she gave birth in 1533 to the daughter who would become Elizabeth I. King Henry had desperately wanted a male heir.

young to understand anything of the world beyond the nursery, but the gentlewomen who watched over and cared for her were perfectly aware of the fact that a royal child ran the risk of becoming a hostage to fortune. They knew that all was not well between Anne and Henry. The king was growing increasingly impatient with his situation, since Anne had still not produced a son. As long as Catherine of Aragon was alive, however, Henry hesitated to take steps to remove his hard-won second wife. Slowly but surely Anne fell from favour, and the fateful coincidences of January 1536 spelled the beginning of the end.

On January 8, 1536, Catherine of Aragon died, and on January 27, the day of her funeral, Anne presented Henry with a stillborn child. Her husband's religious nature, combined with his tendency toward superstition, persuaded him once again to see the hand of God behind misfortune. A mere three months later Anne was accused of having been unfaithful and of plotting with her lovers to kill the king. Never averse to finding a religious excuse for his devious political machina-

**In the company of fellow clerics, Cardinal Wolsey, Henry VIII's trusted aide and one of Europe's most powerful diplomats, casts a dark look as his sovereign tenderly courts Anne Boleyn, who was to be Henry's queen, the mother of Elizabeth I, and, finally, a victim of Henry's executioner.**

tions, Henry claimed that he had been "seduced by witchcraft". Now that he was head of church and state, securing the necessary annulment of his marriage presented no problems. On May 17, 1536, the five men accused of having been Anne's lovers were beheaded. Anne's death was delayed until May 19, since Henry had graciously agreed to her request that she be put to death by an expert swordsman rather than by the traditional stroke of an axe. Since it appeared that there was no English headsman capable of doing the job efficiently with a sword, Henry sent to France for an executioner with the requisite skills.

With the annulment of the marriage, Elizabeth became officially illegitimate, condemned to live in the shadow of her mother's reputation. As she grew older, she felt the humiliation deeply. In fact, as an adult, Elizabeth would never speak of her mother.

Ten days after Anne's death, Henry took his third wife, despite the people's disapproval of his speedy remarriage and the merrymaking which preceded it. His new wife was Jane Seymour, a young woman to whom he had first begun paying considerable attention in the summer of 1534, when she had been one of Anne Boleyn's ladies in waiting. The fact that Henry was already considering her as a possible future bride a mere 10 months after Elizabeth's birth demonstrates the speed with which his hostility to Anne Boleyn had hardened. In 1537 Jane bore him the son for whom he longed and then quietly died soon after childbirth.

By this time Elizabeth's official illegitimacy had caused a drastic decline in her circumstances. Her governess, Lady Bryan, confronted with Henry's complete indifference to his daughter's situation and the resulting lack of servants and supplies, wrote in desperation to Thomas Cromwell, Henry's Lord Privy Seal and greatest henchman. The mighty politician responded sympathetically, and soon Elizabeth's household expanded and came to constitute the kind of surroundings appropriate for a princess.

In 1537, aged four, the little girl began her formal education and made excellent progress right from the outset. A courtier who delivered Henry's Christmas greetings to Elizabeth in 1539 returned to his master able to report that his daughter was quite precocious and had received him as graciously as any great lady. The kindness shown to the young princess by her servants and tutors, allied with her natural intelligence, greatly aided the growth of that self-confidence and strength of character which she would display to the world in the years ahead. She would prove to be her father's daughter in more ways than Henry might ever have expected.

Henry's impatience to get himself a son now seems ironic. Strangely enough, he was the only English sovereign to have all his children reign in succession after him. It was not his son Edward, however, but Elizabeth, the greatest disappointment at birth, who would prove his most memorable and extraordinary heir. She was to rule for more than 44 years and give her name to the Elizabethan Age, one of the most dazzling and creative periods in English history.

Jane Seymour (1509–1537) was the third wife of Henry VIII. Like her predecessor, Anne Boleyn, Queen Jane would pay for her crown with her life; she died after giving birth to the last Tudor prince of Wales, who was crowned King Edward VI in 1547.

# 2

# Perils of an Heir

As Elizabeth grew to girlhood, Henry VIII, once an appealing and vigorous man, gradually became a cruel tyrant and huge glutton. In 1540 he married a European princess, Anne of Cleves, for purely political reasons. Henry's rush to conclude the marriage meant that he had no opportunity to meet his prospective bride prior to the preparations for the wedding. When Anne finally arrived in England it became apparent that the portrait of the princess which Henry had seen greatly flattered her, and the disappointed king soon let it be known that he thought her about as pretty as a "Flanders mare". He quickly divorced the hapless Anne and married Catherine Howard, who proceeded to betray Henry's faith in her by indulging in flagrant immorality. In so behaving she virtually signed her own death warrant. Few people were surprised when Henry had her beheaded in 1542.

In the summer of 1543 the 10-year-old Elizabeth came to court from her own household in the country. All three of the king's children gathered for the celebration of Henry's sixth marriage, to Catherine Parr, which turned out to be his last.

Queen Catherine became as much of a mother as Elizabeth ever knew. She supervised and encouraged Elizabeth's education, along with a number of other

*Much suspected, by me*
*Nothing proved can be*
*Quoth Elizabeth, prisoner*
—rhyme scratched on a window at Woodstock Palace and traditionally ascribed to Elizabeth

King Henry VIII of England and his six queens. Clockwise, from top centre, they are: Anne of Cleves (No. 4); Catherine Howard (No. 5); Anne Boleyn (No. 2); Catherine of Aragon (No. 1); Catherine Parr (No. 6); and Jane Seymour (No. 3).

The young princess Elizabeth, like her father, was a firm believer in physical as well as intellectual exercise, which may have contributed to her remarkable longevity at a time when disease and primitive medical practices doomed many people to an early death.

**Nine-year-old Edward, son of Henry VIII and Jane Seymour, and half-brother of Elizabeth and Mary, became King Edward VI when his father died in 1547. Always frail, Edward was further weakened by measles and smallpox; he died after a six-year reign.**

**In 1540 Anne of Cleves (1515–1557), daughter of a German Protestant duke, became the fourth wife of Henry VIII, who expected the union to strengthen his hand against the Catholic emperor, Charles V. Repelled by his bride, whose beauty had been much exaggerated by painter Hans Holbein, Henry ended the marriage after six months.**

young noblewomen's. Elizabeth's tutors were amazed at her skill and intelligence.

By the time she was five years old, Elizabeth had learned to read and write, and had already begun to study Latin, which she would learn to speak as well as read. For a while Elizabeth shared her half-brother Edward's tutor, but then she graduated to her own. She read and translated classical Greek and Latin authors, and was introduced to French, Spanish, and Italian. Music and devotional studies rounded off her education, along with needlework, which all young gentlewomen had to master.

Elizabeth spent much of her adolescence in study. In one of her portraits she is shown standing with a book in her long white hands, and with another volume open behind her. With her red-blonde hair, pale skin, and intent stare, she looked both modest and regal.

After Henry's death in 1547, Elizabeth went to live with the widowed queen. Henry's will left Elizabeth third in line of succession to the throne. Nine-year-old Edward became king, although actual power lay in the hands of his uncle, Edward Seymour, who had made himself sole protector.

Meanwhile Elizabeth became caught up in the secrecy and intrigue surrounding Catherine's marriage to the protector's handsome brother, Thomas Seymour, a magnetic and ambitious man who was eager to increase his personal prestige and influence. Marrying a person in a high position was one way to attain such ends. Although Seymour had courted Catherine before, Henry VIII had intervened. Seymour did not approach her again until he failed to win approval from the royal council to marry either of the young King Edward's half-sisters.

Now he and Elizabeth were part of the same household. Seymour took to bursting into her bedroom early in the morning, once or twice together with Catherine, but more often without. While at first Catherine may have considered his attention just a playful game, she soon became jealous. Even Elizabeth's governess, Kat Ashley, who had a soft spot for Seymour, grew anxious about the brewing scandal. When one day Catherine surprised them and discovered Seymour embracing the young princess, Elizabeth left the household immediately.

No doubt Elizabeth was flattered by Seymour's overtures. She blushed when his name was mentioned, for she knew he wanted to marry her. Yet she became annoyed as well, aware that he was threatening her reputation as a young woman and a princess.

After Catherine died while giving birth to a child in 1548, Seymour turned his full attention to Elizabeth. Kat Ashley favoured the match and London buzzed with rumours. "The voice goes there", Kat told Elizabeth, "that he shall marry you." However, Seymour still needed the council's permission. If Elizabeth married without it, she would forfeit her right to the throne. When Seymour appealed to her to help his case, she refused, for she felt that his wheeling and dealing had a desperate, untrustworthy edge.

And ultimately her misgivings were shown to be justified. Thomas Seymour, Admiral of the English fleet, was found guilty of treason in 1549. Investigators discovered that not only had he intended to lead an armed uprising against his brother, Edward Seymour, protector of England and guardian of the young King Edward VI, but had also defrauded the government of a vast amount of money in order to finance the conspiracy.

Kat Ashley and another of Elizabeth's servants were rushed away to London where they were held in custody for questioning. Alone, the 15-year-old Elizabeth faced an interrogator who demanded to know whether her servants had advised her to marry Seymour without the council's permission, for this too could be considered treasonable. For days she refused to reveal anything. Then, in shock, she was shown her servant's confessions. They had given in under pressure. Elizabeth read the pages, her heart in her throat, but soon realized that since their confessions did not amount to treason, neither would hers.

While she had resolutely withstood the tense and trying weeks of questioning, Elizabeth was forced to realize how her love and flirtations could never be

**Catherine Parr (1512–1548) was Henry's VIII's sixth wife and the only one to outlive him. Fond of marriage herself —Henry was her third husband, and she married again after his death—Catherine survived her four years as Henry's queen by maintaining silence about religious and political matters.**

**Catherine Howard (1520–1542), who became Henry's fifth queen in 1540, delighted the king with her good looks. Discovering that she shared her charms with others, however, King Henry ordered his unfaithful queen and her lovers executed.**

Dominating London's sky-line in the 16th century was the magnificent St Paul's Church, whose spire was destroyed by lightning in 1561. St Paul's was not exclusively a religious centre in Elizabeth's day. It also served as a market-place and as a meeting ground where her courtiers discussed affairs of state.

*I humbly crave to speak with your highness, which I would not be so bold as to desire if I knew not myself most clear, as I know myself most true.*

—ELIZABETH
in a letter to her sister, Queen Mary, while in captivity on suspicion of involvement in plots against the queen

separated from politics, and how potentially dangerous that could be.

The mere fact of his brother's treachery eventually proved fatal to Edward Seymour, who who was deposed from his position as protector in 1550 and executed in 1552, accused of having conspired against his successor, the duke of Northumberland.

Shortly after his accession to the protectorate, Northumberland granted Hatfield House to Elizabeth as a mark of his respect for her. A magnificent residence standing in beautiful grounds and boasting a well-stocked deer park, Hatfield became Elizabeth's main base of operations. Although she had by now become increasingly popular with the people of London and southeastern England, she remained aware of the fact that her place in line of succession to the throne was by no means assured. By 1551 King Edward's health was failing fast, and he and his ministers of state were becoming increasingly concerned with the succession issue.

Although according to Henry's will Mary was the rightful heir, Edward and his councillors saw her differently—as an unmarried woman and a Catholic who threatened to undo the Protestant reforms of the previous 20 years. It became increasingly obvious that a major political storm was about to break. Before his illness had become serious, Edward had decided that the crown should go to the male heirs of Lady Jane Grey, great-granddaughter of Henry VII, in the event that he died childless. Early in 1553, convinced that he had little time left, he revised his provisions regarding the succession and announced that Jane Grey herself would become queen upon his death.

The wily Northumberland had already foreseen such an eventuality, and had married off his own son to Jane Grey several weeks before Edward's final pronouncement. He had also persuaded one of his closest political allies to marry Jane's sister, Catherine. Such blatant angling for political supremacy served to put Mary, the rightful heir, firmly on her guard. When Edward died on July 6, 1553, she was fully prepared to fight for her inheritance. Drawing on her popularity as the legitimate heir under the terms of Henry's will, she found a vast following among the nobility, and Northumberland's resistance collapsed just two weeks after Edward's death.

Elizabeth now found herself in a dangerous position, as assumed heir and a Protestant under Mary's Catholic rule. Any opposition, or worse, conspiracy, would naturally point to her. Even if she did nothing, she could not stop people from rallying in her name. While she was aware of her growing popularity, she would simply have to use all her powers not to attract suspicion.

Mary's stated intention to repair the breach with Rome and make England Catholic again aroused much controversy throughout the country. Many English churchmen, while not entirely opposed to Mary's suggestions, refused to countenance anything more than a compromise reunion. They hoped that any future agreement would leave in place most of the reforms enacted under Henry VIII and Edward VI. Such a solution suddenly seemed completely impossible, however, when in October 1553 Mary announced that she planned to marry Prince Philip, heir to the Spanish throne and son of Charles V, that same Holy Roman emperor who had forbidden Pope Clement VII to grant Henry a divorce in 1527. Indeed, it was Charles who first proposed to Mary that she should marry Philip. The European Catholic establishment still believed that there was a chance to bring England back into the fold of the faithful, and achieving this by marriage was obviously

As guardian of his nephew, young King Edward VI, Edward Seymour was for two years king of England in everything but name. Under his benevolent regime, freedom of speech and of the press increased.

Thomas Seymour (1508-1549) schemed to displace his older brother Edward (1506–1552) as England's protector, and to marry Princess Elizabeth. He also tried to arrange a marriage between Lady Jane Grey and the young Edward VI.

Lady Jane Grey (1537–1554), the innocent victim of a plot to prevent Mary from gaining the throne following the death of Edward VI, was proclaimed queen of England in 1553. Deposed after 10 days, she was imprisoned in the Tower of London and, at the age of 17, beheaded at Mary's vengeful behest.

greatly preferable to forcing the issue by war.

Under the terms of the proposed marriage treaty Philip was to be king but the real executive power would remain with Mary. All appointments to the major offices of church and state would be made by her, and the appointees would be Englishmen. Spanish interference in English affairs was out of the question, and the treaty would in no way compromise England's existing commitments abroad.

Inevitably, many people thought these assurances insufficient. The leaders of a nationwide plot wrote to Elizabeth of their plans to revolt and put her on the throne. Would she support them? Elizabeth refused to give them a straight answer and wisely put nothing at all in writing.

When the insurrection broke out in January 1554, Mary ordered Elizabeth to London despite the fact that she was sick. To Mary, of course, Elizabeth's illness seemed an excuse to keep out of trouble. As she approached London, Elizabeth had the curtains of her litter pulled back so that the people could see her—pale and swollen, but proud and defiant. It was a display calculated to show that she had nothing to hide.

The pace of debate in Mary's council became feverish as the gathered members discussed the options regarding Elizabeth. They realized that killing her might spark further widespread turmoil. Admittedly, the government had successfully crushed a previous rebellion staged by a handful of nobles and their retainers, but the prospect of dealing with a nation in arms bent on avenging the death of its beloved Elizabeth unnerved them. As it was, they had no evidence of treason on Elizabeth's part, and none of them was prepared to be responsible for her custody. Unable to reach agreement on the charges that might be made against Elizabeth, the assembled officials decided to confine her to the Tower.

When two councillors came to escort her on her trip down the Thames, she begged them to let her talk, or at least write, to Mary. She found it hard to believe that this had been Mary's own decision. Elizabeth's pen scratched slowly across the page as she swore her innocence and pleaded with Mary to see her—to spare her life. When she had finished, she drew diagonal lines across the rest of the page so that no forger could tamper with her words. Regardless, Elizabeth's letter only succeeded in rousing Mary to a fury.

A cold rain fell as the royal boatmen rowed Elizabeth's barge down the Thames River on March 18, 1554. Approaching the city, Elizabeth turned pale at the sight of London Bridge, which was now adorned with tall poles on top of which the heads of recently executed traitors were fast decomposing. The sunken, sightless eyes stared down upon the captive princess. The silent message in their shrivelled mouths was that there is no such thing as partial success in opposing a monarch. Each side in such conflicts stands to lose everything.

"Bear witness that I come here not as a traitor," Elizabeth said as she disembarked at the river entrance to the Tower. For two months she lived without books or any news of the outer world, dreading that here her life would end as her mother's had. But then, on May 19, she was hurried away without explanation, and she feared that Mary had decided to have her murdered secretly.

But in fact, Mary had found a guardian for her half-sister. Elizabeth's journey to further imprisonment, however, looked more like a royal procession. As she made her way under guard through the countryside, crowds gathered to cheer her and bells pealed from churches.

In July 1554 Philip arrived in England, and he and Mary were married in Winchester cathedral. The weather for the occasion was abysmal, and the constant rain soaked Philip to the skin during his ride from the coast. Throughout the proceedings Philip could only shiver in his sodden clothes while his bride fixed her stare upon the sacrament, seemingly refusing to look at him. Mary looked older than he had expected and, in the eyes of his courtiers, seemed excessively pious and insufficiently acquainted with the latest fashions. By the end of the day most of the naturally flamboyant and showy Spaniards were joking cruelly at Mary's

The Duke of Northumberland (1502–1553) became protector of the realm after he deposed (and later executed) Edward Seymour. Unlike Seymour, Northumberland was a harsh ruler who curtailed personal freedom and ordered numerous executions. In 1553, however, having failed to place Lady Jane Grey on the throne, he was himself beheaded on the orders of Queen Mary.

Queen Mary I (1516–1558) confirms her pledge to marry Prince Philip of Spain (1527-1598). Eager to restore Roman Catholicism to England, Mary saw the powerful and devoutly Catholic Philip as the perfect match, but the marriage was bitterly opposed by her advisors, her Parliament, and her people.

expense, much to Philip's dismay. One described her as "old and flabby", while another went so far as to say "It would take God himself to drink this cup." It was not an auspicious start to a marriage upon which Catholicism had pinned so many hopes.

After 10 months of confinement in the gatehouse of Woodstock, a run-down royal hunting lodge in Oxfordshire, Elizabeth returned quietly to court in 1555. Her release was largely due to the personal intervention of Philip, who was eager to stay on good terms with the young woman who would eventually succeed Mary. For her part, Elizabeth realized that Philip was her best protection at court, and consequently did her best to charm him. Mary gave little thought to these diplomatic exchanges between her husband and her half-sister, since she had by now become convinced that she was pregnant with an heir of her own.

As the summer of 1555 progressed it became apparent that the queen, far from being with child, was seriously ill. Increasingly, she withdrew into herself, rejecting the company of her husband and the entire court, spending whole days sitting alone and speaking to no one. Finally, realizing that his pious and boring wife was past all hopes of child-bearing, Philip lost patience. Since there was now no prospect of an heir, Spain and the Holy Roman Empire could gain nothing by his continued presence in England. On August 29, 1555, he returned to Europe.

In the years following Philip's departure, Elizabeth simply watched and waited. Increasingly, senior officials in Mary's government made the journey from London to Elizabeth's various country residences in order to become acquainted with the self-assured and quick-witted young woman who would one day become queen.

In Elizabeth's eyes, Mary's reign emerged as a lesson in regality gone wrong, a perfect example of how not to order the affairs of England. The Protestant reforms enacted under her father and her half-brother had become firmly entrenched in English society, and the first signs of a new national consciousness were becoming apparent. Despite Mary's determination to make England officially Catholic again, to put the clock back 30 years, it was obvious that England's political and spiritual separation from Europe had become inevitable.

Mary had lost the support of both her councillors and her people by marrying an unpopular and unaffectionate foreign prince, thus risking English security and sovereignty. Her burning of Protestants had only strengthened their cause. In 1557 Philip made a brief reappearance on the English scene. Although he and Mary had been separated for two years by this time, the marriage was still legally in

Although Mary Tudor ascended to the throne on a wave of popularity, by the end of her five-year reign she was hated by almost everyone, largely because of her persecution of Protestants and her marriage to Philip, which reduced England to the virtual status of a Spanish colony.

**Elizabeth, imprisoned in the Tower, is approached by the guards who escorted her on her daily walks along the Tower wall, from which she saw prisoners executed. Unaware that Mary would never risk beheading her popular half-sister, Elizabeth expected each day to be her last.**

effect and Philip had come to cash in on its political importance.

War had broken out between the Holy Roman Empire and France, and Philip, as a member of the ruling imperial dynasty, the Hapsburgs, was eager to exploit his marriage alliance in order to bring England into the conflict on the imperial side. Although this made a mockery of the terms of their marriage contract, which had precluded Spain from influencing English foreign policy, Mary was delighted by the mere fact of Philip's renewed interest in her and immediately forced her councillors to issue a declaration of war.

She had been visibly much happier than usual during the weeks of Philip's visit to England, although as far as Philip was concerned the negotiations were strictly business. On June 7, 1557, Philip sailed for France, taking his leave of Mary for the last time. His early successes in the campaign did England little good, since they made him over-confident and, consequently, extremely careless. The French soon gained the upper hand and captured England's last possession in Europe, the trading port of Calais.

Mary's political fortunes and personal happiness now reached their lowest point ever, and, as a result, her health began to fail. By 1558 Elizabeth's country household had already become a shadow court as preparations were made for the eventual transfer of power. A breathless, expectant atmosphere reigned. At last, on November 17, news of Mary's death arrived. At the age of 25, Elizabeth had survived her long and difficult path to the throne. Bells rang out across the land. Bonfires blazed throughout London, as they had at her birth. And in the streets people drank to the new queen's health.

**Protestants are executed in the reign of Mary, a devout Catholic who would be remembered as "Bloody Mary" because of the 300 "heretics" burned at the stake while she was queen. Such persecution helped create much revulsion in England against Rome.**

# 3

# Her Princely Majesty

On January 15, 1559, in her litter draped with cloth of gold, wearing splendid robes, and with her tawny hair unbound, the new queen glittered as she rode from the once-dreaded Tower to her coronation in Westminster abbey. A light snow fell on the packed London streets, dusting the heads of the crowds. "God save your grace," the people cheered as she passed by. "God save you all", Elizabeth replied. "I thank you with all my heart."

Along the route pageants had been prepared, and after a welcoming speech by the Lord Mayor, Elizabeth turned to the crowd. "Be ye assured that I will be as good to you as ever queen was unto her people", she said. If Elizabeth's mother had left her a shadowy reputation, Elizabeth always prided herself on being "totally English", and she never stopped extolling her love for her people—in return for their love for her.

After the coronation ceremony, Elizabeth sat down to a lavish banquet that lasted for 10 hours. According to tradition, the queen's champion, fully armed, rode into the hall on his horse. There he

Elizabeth is crowned queen of England in 1558. No one at the time could have predicted that the slender 25-year-old would give her name to an exhilarating age celebrated for its theatre, music, literature, natural sciences, expanded sea power, rising prosperity, religious tolerance, and rapid industrial growth.

The great seal of Queen Elizabeth. When she was crowned, few diplomats in England or abroad believed Elizabeth would actually govern her realm. Within a month of her coronation, however, the Spanish ambassador reported that she was feared and obeyed exactly as her father, the formidable and strong-willed Henry VIII, had been.

John Knox (1505–1572) harangues ladies of the Scottish court. A fiery and fanatical Calvinist, Knox ignited a Protestant revolt against the Catholic French when he arrived in Scotland in 1559. The brilliant diplomacy of Elizabeth and her secretary of state, William Cecil (1529–1598), however, averted war and produced the Treaty of Edinburgh, which ended French claims to the Scottish succession.

threw down his gauntlet and challenged to battle anyone who denied Elizabeth's right to the throne.

Beneath all the pageantry, Elizabeth faced a difficult situation when she became queen. Everyone assumed that she, like her sister Mary, would quickly marry and soon produce an heir. Few anticipated that she herself would actually attempt to govern.

"Women are unsuited to rule," thundered John Knox, the Scottish Protestant leader in *The First Blast of the Trumpet Against the Monstrous Regiment of Women*. It was quite a title, even though "monstrous regiment" meant "unnatural rule" in the English of that time.

Knox's blustering pamphlet was directed against Elizabeth's half-sister Mary and the two Marys in Scotland, the regent Mary of Lorraine who governed for her daughter. Mary, Queen of Scots. By an odd quirk of fate, late 16th-century Europe saw an abundance of queens: as well as Elizabeth and her half-sister in England, and the two Marys in Scotland, there was the highly influential queen mother Catherine de Médici, the behind-the-scenes ruler for three of her sons in France.

Unfortunately for Knox, his pamphlet appeared in the first year of Elizabeth's reign, just when he and his followers needed Elizabeth's support. The Scottish Protestants were mounting a rebellion to oust the powerful Catholic French from their country.

Hastily, Knox declared Elizabeth a divine exception. Elizabeth likewise saw herself as divinely chosen by right of her succession to the throne, and, as such, different from other women. She was the legitimate heir by birth and blood—she was not *usurping* power.

From the start, she had no intention of giving up her power, even to her carefully chosen councillors. She sought their advice but would make up her own mind. She was also not above blaming them whenever things went wrong. Of her 12 councillors the one whom she trusted most was her diligent, knowledgeable, and shrewd principal secretary, William Cecil.

Cecil shared Elizabeth's political pragmatism, as well as her deep concern for peace and stability. Although she surprised everyone by maintaining sole authority, Elizabeth was not bent on overturning the traditional order. She respected the established social hierarchies, and preferred preservation of the status quo to any kind of change. Not even Cecil was truly comfortable with a woman ruler, yet he and the queen understood one another, and worked closely together for 38 long years.

Elizabeth made it clear that she would not stand for any disobedience, patterning her rule after her father's model of absolute monarchy. People had begun to look back on Henry VIII with more fondness, and Elizabeth did not discourage being compared to him.

While she demanded obedience, she also enjoyed charming men into agreeing with her views.

To ensure that her statesmen and courtiers did not take their positions for granted, Elizabeth alternated between outbursts of royal displeasure and displays of humour and warmth. She also made

**William Cecil, Elizabeth's principal secretary of state, was a clever and cautious advisor and administrator. He organized a network of spies to ferret out plots against the queen and took responsibility for the execution of Mary, Queen of Scots. Queen Elizabeth frequently referred to him as "Sir Spirit".**

Mary Stuart, queen of Scotland (1542–1587), a Catholic and a direct descendant of Henry VIII, was next in line for England's throne after Elizabeth and the instigator of many plots to overthrow her. Imprisoned in England for 19 years, she was finally beheaded for approving a plan to assassinate Elizabeth.

sure that discussion of royal matters did not extend beyond her circle of advisors. For sure, there would be no talking about affairs of state with her ladies-in-waiting.

The war with France, which Elizabeth inherited from Mary, brought out her two most pressing concerns: marriage and religion. She needed European allies, such as the Spanish, and she certainly did not need more enemies.

Philip, Mary's widower and current king of Spain, presented himself as Elizabeth's first suitor. Throughout the courts of Europe, the people accepted him, and it was generally assumed that he would one day marry Elizabeth, who badly needed his support. But finally she told him politely that their mutual interests could be insured without marriage.

Delaying, moving slowly, and hiding her real intentions were tactics that Elizabeth had learned during her unsettled years under Mary. Now they served her well as queen. She waited until there was peace with France before making England a Protestant state. But even then, her religious policies kept to a moderate course in the hope of satisfying as many different beliefs as possible.

Some called the queen's church "a leaden mediocrity". Inevitably, she found it impossible to satisfy both the Catholics and the Protestants. The Puritans, the most radical Protestants in England, were angry because they had counted on Elizabeth to introduce much stronger reforms. They hungered for the establishment of a church in England which would bear little resemblance to the Catholic Church. They wanted their Christianity stripped of those aspects of Catholic doctrine and ritual which the Reformation movement so fiercely opposed. Although loyal to her as a Protestant queen, they continued to pressure her throughout her reign.

The Virgin Queen, as Elizabeth was called, glitters in her elaborately jewelled white gown as courtiers transport her to a wedding. Elizabeth thoroughly enjoyed opportunities to be seen, and she was most fond of weddings—as long as they had her approval.

# 4

# Rumours of Love

Early in 1559, one young man in particular suddenly sprang into prominence at court. Robert Dudley, son of the highly ambitious duke of Northumberland, who had been powerful during Edward's reign, was appointed Elizabeth's "master of the horse". The two had known each other since childhood, and under Mary had resided in the Tower at the same time. In the coronation procession he had marched behind her, leading her charger.

Now people began to talk about how much time Elizabeth and Dudley were spending together, and how openly affectionate the queen was toward him. Dudley was married, although his ailing wife lived in the country and never came to court.

No doubt Elizabeth was attracted to Dudley's energy, athletic prowess, and skill at conversation. They shared a wide range of interests, and Elizabeth delighted in the way he organized court

**Robert Dudley (1533—1588) was Elizabeth's long-time intimate friend, although she sometimes teased him about his "bad blood" (his father and grandfather had both been beheaded for treason), and she firmly maintained her superior role. "I will", she once insisted to him, "have here but one mistress and no master."**

**Elizabeth's formal portraits reveal much about the fashions of her period. Here, her flared, richly ornamented dress is extended by a farthingale, a canvas petticoat supported by a frame hung from the waist. As she aged, Elizabeth rarely smiled, afraid of cracking the very thick make-up she wore to look younger.**

entertainments for her. She was also willing to ignore his less than reputable family history. For Elizabeth, part of his appeal stemmed from the fact that, because he was already married, she could spend time with him without having to commit herself. There was no need to decide whether or not to marry. However, this did not stop her from taking a perverse delight in provoking scandal.

Whatever the truth, the courts of France and Spain were scandalized by the exaggerated rumours they heard about Elizabeth's behaviour. It appeared that the English queen was doing nothing but seeing her married horsemaster. Kat Ashley, now mistress of the queen's maids, begged Elizabeth to end all the rumours by marrying one of her suitors.

In response, Elizabeth said imperiously that no one could stop her from doing what she wanted. "If she ever had the will or had found pleasure in such a dishonourable life," Elizabeth said to Kat, "from which God preserve her, she did not know of anyone who could forbid her." And because marriage was

**Elizabeth takes the air in her royal barge. The queen, who liked outdoor activities, often took a brisk walk before breakfast; in 1577 she built a wall around her terrace at Windsor Castle in order "to prevent persons seeing into the queen's walk".**

also a political issue for a queen, she did not want to rush into it. Her councillors and the foreign ambassadors were dismayed and puzzled. Had she been swept away by passion or did she know exactly what she was doing?

Flanked by courtiers, including a knight of the Garter (right), an ermine-robed Elizabeth displays the paraphernalia of regality: on her head is a crown; her left hand holds the orb, a globe bearing a cross; her right hand holds the sceptre signifying power.

Elizabeth's official signature ended with the letter "R", standing for "Regina", or queen. Elizabeth saw herself as the personification of her country; to strengthen that image, she capitalized on her appeal as a woman and, at great expense, maintained a truly magnificent court.

> *When she smiled, it was a pure sunshine that everyone did choose to bask in, if they could; but anon came a storm from a sudden gathering of clouds, and the thunder fell in wondrous manner on all alike.*
> —SIR JOHN HARINGTON
> English writer and godson of Elizabeth I

To complicate matters, Dudley's sickly wife, Amy, was found with her neck broken at the bottom of a staircase in a house empty of servants. The obvious assumption was that Dudley had had her murdered. Though Amy Dudley had been suffering from breast cancer and in desperation might have committed suicide, there was no good explanation for why she had been left alone in the house. Nonetheless, Dudley was eventually cleared.

Dudley, although free, remained an object of suspicion, and was widely seen as an ambitious upstart. Elizabeth would have to decide how serious she was about him. Was she or was she not prepared to marry him? She drew up the document that would make him an earl, since only a member of the nobility could marry the queen, but before signing it, she slashed the paper to pieces with a knife.

Neither did Dudley know which way to turn. After doing everything he could to regain Elizabeth's favour, he was frustrated by her indecision and by the fact that he could not force her will.

If she was not about to marry, Elizabeth's councillors told her, and they hoped she would not marry Dudley, then she should at least name a successor. Naming a successor, Elizabeth replied, was asking for trouble. She did not want anyone to be a focus for rebellion during her own reign as she had been in Mary's.

The succession issue reached crisis proportions when in the autumn of 1562 Elizabeth caught smallpox. It was only the fourth year of her reign, and England was in the midst of renewed war with France, unsuccessfully trying to win back the port of Calais which Mary had lost to the French in 1558.

In the 16th century smallpox often attacked court, city, and country, leaving many people dead or hideously pockmarked. Mary Sidney, who caught the disease while nursing the queen, was so badly disfigured that she withdrew from court for life. After the queen had burned with fever for a week, the spots appeared and, in accordance with the medical practice of the time, she was wrapped in red cloth to prevent scarring. And red cloth was draped over all the windows of her room. For a while not even Elizabeth thought she would live. However, she did survive, and fortunately her pockmarks, when salved with creams and covered with make-up, were noticeable but not disfiguring.

In the council chamber, her advisors met desperately to discuss possible successors. Ironically enough, most were women. Catherine Grey, like her executed sister Lady Jane Grey, was English, Protestant, and married. Unfortunately, she had married secretly, without royal permission, which was considered treason. As a punishment, Elizabeth had angrily shut Catherine and her husband in the Tower.

The young Mary Queen of Scots had a legitimate claim, which Elizabeth recognized even though Mary's line had been excluded from the will of Henry VIII. On the other hand, Mary was not English, but a Scot and, worst of all, had been raised as a French Catholic. The question of succession was still not answered.

Elizabeth, an avid horse-woman all her life, addresses her troops at Tilbury. A few months before she died, Elizabeth rode ten miles and then went hunting; a court observer reported that the queen, despite her age, moved "briskly as though she was 18 years old".

# 5

# Trouble from the North

Mary Stuart returned to Scotland as queen in 1561, leaving behind her familiar France. She had not only grown up there but had briefly been queen until her adolescent husband's early death. The Scottish leaders coolly greeted this tall, auburn-haired, foreign-sounding 18-year-old. At six feet tall, a height which would have made an ordinary woman an oddity, it gave to Mary a striking regal authority.

A Catholic queen returning as a stranger to her Protestant kingdom, Mary needed Elizabeth's support. Yet as a Catholic, Mary refused to give up her claim to be the true queen of England. This infuriated Elizabeth. Although the two queens kept planning face-to-face meetings, each attempt was called off.

To further complicate matters, Mary was a potential successor to Elizabeth's throne. For both Mary and Elizabeth marriage was a crucial political issue, and Elizabeth took great interest in Mary's marriage prospects. Elizabeth did not want Mary to wed a foreign Catholic prince who might support Mary's claim to the English throne, and thus threaten to invade England and depose her.

**Elizabeth had hundreds of extravagantly decorated dresses like this one, but she wore such finery only when she appeared in public. In private, she preferred simple garments, and sometimes wore the same plain and simple dress for five days in succession.**

**Lord Darnley (1545–1567) charmed Mary of Scotland, who married him quickly, a move she later regretted. Her secretary wrote that it was "heartbreak to (Mary) to think he should be her husband", and that she longed to find a way "to be free of him".**

Mary, Queen of Scots, arrives in Scotland in 1561. The
death of Mary's husband, Francis II (1544—1560) broke
the link between Scotland and France, which pleased
Elizabeth, but she was disturbed by the knowledge that
Mary would now claim the crown of Scotland and possibly
that of England as well.

Elizabeth hit upon a surprising solution, not only to the problem of Mary's marriage but to her own: Mary should marry the queen's favourite, Dudley. If she could count on anyone, Elizabeth could count on Dudley to remain loyal to her and not plot a rebellion. In addition, she would agree to make Mary and Dudley's children her heirs.

In a lavish ceremony in front of the Scotish ambassador, Elizabeth took the essential first step and made Dudley earl of Leicester. Though no one could quite believe it, it seemed that she was prepared to give up her closest companion to another woman, by reputation one of the most beautiful in Europe.

Marrying off Dudley and Mary, and thus resolving the succession issue, would lessen the need for Elizabeth to marry. The pressure did not entirely disappear, however. To her councillors, it was inconceivable that at 31 Elizabeth might intend never to marry. Delegations from other suitors came and went—envoys from Archduke Charles of Austria, and representatives of the Swedish crown, dressed in doublets adorned with red velvet hearts pierced by arrows.

Mary's Scottish ambassador, for one, saw through all Elizabeth's procrastination and evasion. "I know the truth of that, madam," Melville told her. "Your majesty thinks, if you were married you would be but queen of England; and now you are both king and queen. I know your spirit cannot endure a commander."

From her own perspective, Elizabeth's solution to the dilemma may have been neat and tidy, but it did present certain problems. Not surprisingly, Mary felt as though she were being given Elizabeth's hand-me-downs and was insulted. And Dudley, the new earl of Leicester, did not want to be sent packing while he still believed he had a chance to win Elizabeth's hand. He convinced Elizabeth to let the young Catholic Lord Darnley, another possible English husband for Mary, go to Scotland. Elizabeth realized her mistake too late. Infatuated with Darnley and his youthful good looks. Mary promptly married him in 1565.

**Elizabeth, perhaps considering the question of marriage, converses with one of her ladies-in-waiting. Urged by her councillors to wed, Elizabeth remained evasive, but Dudley once revealed that on many occasions she had declared, "I will never marry."**

Relations between Elizabeth and Leicester grew shaky. Without the queen's favour, Leicester was virtually nothing, with no family honour or fortune to fall back on. While he had plenty of followers, his numerous enemies at court were ready to leap on him. He knew not "what to hope or fear, what to do or what to think". Did he have any hope of marrying the queen?

Cecil opposed a marriage to Leicester and bluntly told Elizabeth so. She would gain nothing from the match, Cecil argued, and "he is like to prove unkind or jealous of the queen's majesty". Elizabeth probably recognized this. "I will have here but one mistress and no master", she yelled at him on one occasion in front of the whole court.

Elizabeth's insistence on having her own way was beginning to meet with opposition. An unmarried queen who looked as though she might remain single was bad enough, but one who refused to relinquish her control to the men in her government was too much. Her intelligence was widely acknowledged, but, while Elizabeth's wavering tactics may now appear successful, to those men responsible for

An Elizabethan chamber orchestra. Herself a performer and composer, the monarch enthusiastically supported both sacred and secular music. She kept many musicians at her court and often arranged for free public concerts, so that even the poor could enjoy her favourite art.

administering policy they seemed a mixture of hopeless indecision and lack of direction.

The royal council was the centre of political power in Elizabeth's time, not Parliament, as it is today. While council members met daily, Parliament met every few years, and only when Elizabeth called for it. All bills had to be approved by the queen, and freedom of speech was severely limited, against which the Puritan members of Parliament protested repeatedly as an infringement of their basic rights.

In 1566 both houses of Parliament, the Commons and the Lords, joined together to insist on the right to discuss the succession issue. They worried about

**Mary, Queen of Scots, is serenaded by David Rizzio (1533–1566), an Italian musician who came to her court as a singer in 1561. He soon gained her affection and eventually rose to a position of great power and influence as her unofficial secretary of state.**

Mary, Queen of Scots, signs her abdication in 1567 after her marriage to the Protestant Bothwell had provoked the Catholic Scottish nobles to rebellion. Escaping her subsequent imprisonment, she raised an army of 6,000 men, but was defeated in 1568 and took refuge in England.

The earl of Bothwell (1536-1578), who masterminded the murder of Mary's husband, Darnley, and then kidnapped the queen and persuaded her to marry him. Driven from Scotland by the nobility, he fled to Denmark, where he was imprisoned by the Danish king, and died insane 10 years later.

Elizabeth's health—a woman so thin and tense, they thought, might not live very long. If Elizabeth refused, they would withhold a grant to collect taxes, which Parliament controlled. And Elizabeth needed more money.

Their slightly built but dynamic and vocal queen was furious. She turned on one of the highest-ranking members and called him a traitor. Of all the men, she expected Leicester to support her cause, but he could only lamely say that he would readily die at her feet. She fumed. That had nothing to do with the matter.

Finally Elizabeth had her way, and nothing was decided about the succession. As for marriage, she was still negotiating with the Austrian archduke, wasn't she? Nevertheless. it had proven a tough battle.

Meanwhile, in Scotland, Mary was providing an example of how a queen who shared Elizabeth's passion and energy but lacked her self-control could undo herself through marriage. It turned out that the boyish Darnley had another side—drunken, brutish, and overbearing. Mary longed to be rid of him. Her true affections were being lavished upon her secretary, the Italian David Rizzio.

As her favourite, Rizzio rose quickly to power and was causing the same sort of scandal that Leicester had at Elizabeth's court. Finally Darnley and his accomplices burst in on Mary and Rizzio at dinner, dragged Rizzio from his chair, and stabbed him to death. Soon afterwards, Darnley's house was blown up and his body found in the garden. The power-hungry earl of Bothwell, who had plotted Darnley's murder, allegedly with Mary's approval, was cleared in a sham inquest. After a speedy divorce from his wife, the earl forced Mary to marry him.

In disgust, the Scottish nobles revolted, taking Mary prisoner. At their command, she abdicated in favour of her one-year-old son, James. In 1568, after eight months under guard in a lonely castle, Mary escaped to England, cutting off her long hair to avoid detection. She threw herself on Elizabeth's mercy only to find herself imprisoned once again, too dangerous to be allowed her freedom. However, Mary would end up having a huge impact on English politics for years to come.

---

**Mary, Queen of Scots, fails to save her lover, David Rizzio, from the daggers of an armed band that included her husband, Lord Darnley. The rash and bloody act, perpetrated in 1566, cost the violent and unpredictable Darnley his own life the following year.**

# 6

# Plots and More Plots

$M$ary wanted protection and help to regain her throne. She was not only Elizabeth's cousin, but a woman of royal blood and a queen who ruled by divine right. Her forced abdication set a shocking and unwelcome precedent. On the other hand, she was accused of being unfaithful to her husband and of consenting to his murder.

Elizabeth expressed outrage at the events in Scotland. She could not send an army in Mary's support to Scotland, since that would violate her treaty with the Scottish Protestant leaders. Nor could she send Mary back as a prisoner when Mary had appealed to her for protection. She did not want to let Mary out of England because Mary was certain to head for France, and with French support she might try to take back her Scottish throne, and Elizabeth's as well.

So Elizabeth kept Mary under the eye of a staunchly Protestant and unsympathetic guardian, while a commission was set up to investigate the charges against her. However, Mary continued to be a magnet for trouble.

Though she appeared guilty of involvement in the plot to murder Darnley, the leader of the queen's commission was tempted by a new plot. He, the duke of Norfolk, should marry Mary, proposed William Maitland, Mary's former secretary. For the Scots as well as the English, this would solve the problem of what to do with her.

---

Although Elizabeth had never denied her cousin Mary Stuart's right to the Scottish crown, she regarded Mary, who generally placed her personal fortunes ahead of her country's as an incompetent sovereign.

Thomas Howard, duke of Norfolk (1536–1572), was one of the most prominent men in England, but neither his position nor his immense wealth prevented his execution for treason.

One of the many magnificent horses owned by Elizabeth. The queen's passion for riding may have contributed to her extraordinary good health. Apart from smallpox, her only major ailment was an ulcer in her leg, which briefly forced her to travel, much to her disgust, in a coach.

As England's highest peer and only duke, the 31-year-old Norfolk remained an old feudal-style noble, his imposing wealth and power drawn from his enormous landholdings. On his domains, he was practically a king in his own right, and his town house contained the first indoor bowling alley in England. Wherever he went, he was escorted by 500 retainers on horseback. Although Norfolk was the queen's cousin and was trusted by her to be above petty politicking, he considered himself undervalued by her. He felt upstaged by ambitious new arrivals like Leicester who pushed and charmed their way to wealth and honour.

Norfolk was not alone in favouring his marriage to Mary. A number of Elizabeth's councillors also supported it, including Leicester. They were, they said, ready to help Mary win back her throne if she agreed to the marriage, and they would secure her children the English succession. At last that crucial issue would be resolved.

Once again, the need to have a settled succession seemed urgent. England's relations with Spain had grown tense after Elizabeth seized the contents of three Spanish ships that had entered waters too near to England. Piracy, thundered Spain's King Philip, in vain. Unfortunately for Elizabeth, the Spanish had an army of 10,000 men based in the Netherlands, strategically stationed near to England and posing a threat of invasion.

Elizabeth's councillors had had enough of her indecision and their own subordination to her. Even Leicester, entrusted to inform Elizabeth of any arrangements her council made without her knowledge, lost his nerve and backed out. Though rumours of the proposed marriage raced across the country. Elizabeth decided to confront Norfolk herself. She could coerce him to tell her of the marriage. She even asked him to dine alone with her. But though the queen gave him every chance to confess, Norfolk continued to deny everything.

**Mary and Elizabeth exchange harsh words in 1568. Although Elizabeth addressed Mary as "ma chère soeur" (my beloved sister) and "my dear cousin", she was contemptuous of Mary's political and personal judgment.**

Elizabeth was worried, knowing the wealth and number of men that Norfolk had at his disposal, knowing too that her grip on her other councillors was shaky. Even Leicester could not be absolutely trusted. The Spanish were two days away by ship and England had no standing army. In the north, still a strongly Catholic and fiercely independent part of the country, revolt threatened. Rebels were rallying in support of Norfolk, the Scottish queen, the Catholic cause—or all three.

Even when Elizabeth regained the upper hand with her councillors and imprisoned Norfolk, the northern rebellion erupted in 1569. Bursting into the great Durham cathedral, armed men burned the Protestant English Bible and heard the Latin Catholic mass. However, their main objective, to capture Mary, failed and the rebels were forced to retreat. Elizabeth's consequent punishment of the rebellious north was so harsh that people were dismayed. She could be just as bloody as her father and sister, they whispered.

Three months later, in 1570, Elizabeth was finally excommunicated as a heretic by Pope Pius V.

**Durham cathedral was the first stop for a group of rebellious northern earls and their followers in 1569. Defeated in their subsequent effort to rescue Mary, Queen of Scots, the rebels fled to Scotland, pursued by Elizabeth's armies. Some 800 men were executed, and others lost their lands or were exiled.**

Pope Pius V (1504–1572) was no friend of religious freedom. Besides excommunicating Elizabeth for heresy, he aided the French in their brutal campaign against the Huguenots, and the Spanish in their persecution of Protestants in the Netherlands.

For Catholics, this effectively meant that she had been deposed. Catholic subjects would be disobeying the church if they obeyed "that guilty woman of England".

With this, Elizabeth's attempt at a workable religious conformity crumbled. England lay in a precarious position: a weak, divided country without a European ally. It seemed the queen had lost the peace and stability that she so valued.

Although Elizabeth introduced strict laws against Catholics, she could not stop plots against her. In 1571 she learned of a conspiracy, organized by a Florentine banker named Ridolfi, to put Mary Stuart on the throne. Once again, the gullible, ambitious Norfolk was involved. Ths Spanish supported the coup and stood in the wings, ready to intervene.

This time Norfolk had gone too far. He deserved death as a traitor. And yet he was her cousin, her highest peer. Elizabeth paced her chambers sleeplessly. He had to be executed, Cecil urged. After hesitating for five months, Elizabeth signed his death warrant. And what about Mary, the real cause of unrest? But Mary was a queen. She could not kill Mary.

# 7

# All the Queen's Men

The question of the queen's marriage did not disappear, and Elizabeth's councillors spent more time worrying about this than any other issue during her reign.

Until she was in her mid-40s, and whenever she needed allies in Europe, Elizabeth used her eligibility as a political tool. She would begin negotiating a match with the French royal family to exasperate the Spanish, or favour the archduke of Austria, the cousin of King Philip of Spain, to enrage the French.

Though her councillors begged for her marriage, she mused, they could not agree on the right man. Since there were no likely Protestant foreign candidates, religion remained a problem. So while they could agree that the problem of the succession should be settled, they could not decide who would be the best choice.

Elizabeth was in an unenviable position. If she married, it would be for political reasons, and she would lose her power without gaining personal happiness. By ruling on her own, she had to face continual disapproval and scandal. Most men would not believe that the strong-minded, independent Elizabeth might not *want* to marry. As queen, her confidence in her ability to govern her country well outweighed her feeling of obligation to produce an heir. In addition, she probably also feared the risks

Elizabeth greets Sir Thomas Gresham (1519—1579) at the opening of the Royal Exchange in 1570. Gresham, Europe's shrewdest financier and an expert on the intrinsic value of coinage, was assigned to manage England's finances three days after Elizabeth's accession. It was a wise choice; Elizabeth found his knowledge and abilities invaluable.

> *Sir Christopher Hatton was wont to say that the Queen did fish for men's souls, and had so sweet a bait, that no one could escape her network.*
> —SIR JOHN HARINGTON

Accompanied by courtiers and retainers, Elizabeth goes hawking. Most Elizabethans, including their sovereign, were extremely fond of this sport, in which peregrine falcons, sparrow hawks, and goshawks were used to hunt other birds and small animals.

A 16th-century tapestry pays tribute to music and dance, both immensely popular with Elizabethans. Most secular and religious festivals featured dancing and singing, and many people could play at least one musical instrument. Every large town and noble household liked to maintain its own resident musicians.

Coins issued in Elizabeth's reign carried a monogram composed of the letters in her name. Like heads of state throughout history, Elizabeth I was worried by inflation, which had reached a serious level in England by 1558. Her first important official act was to order currency reform.

of dying in childbirth, as did so many women in her day.

It was rumoured also that she had remained single only so she could indulge in all those secret love affairs.

Elizabeth sought satisfaction in regality as a profession, and worked extraordinarily hard at it. Although she officially retired for the night at nine, Elizabeth often kept working until very late, unable to sleep. As a result, mornings were not her best time of the day. After a quick walk in her private garden, she took breakfast alone, as she did most of her meals. Elizabeth had a small appetite but a terrible sweet tooth.

Dressing was a lengthy procedure for the queen.

Elizabeth had her teeth cleaned with a piece of cloth, a tooth soap, and gold and enamel tooth-picks. She dyed her hair as she grew older, attached additional tresses of false hair, and later wore wigs, as did many women of the time. Her ladies helped her into her eight layers of clothing, and added collars or ruffs, which, until starch was introduced to England in 1564, were held in shape by a frame of tiny sticks. Then they handed her the large pouch that she wore on her waist. As she grew older, Elizabeth would dress in only black and white to set off the sparkling array of her jewels and the vivid red of her hair.

Elizabeth spent her days answering correspondence, reading reports, and meeting individually with her councillors. She set aside some quiet time every day for study, reading, and translating the classics, as she had done since girlhood. She would exercise by walking briskly, by dancing, and if she was in the country, by hunting. She was also a fine musician and singer who wrote her own pieces. She loved the glorious church music composed for her Chapel Royal.

The young, unmarried maids of honour, sent to

Surrounded by members of her court, Elizabeth is borne in her plumed litter. Among those responsible for the queen's safety were members of a group known as the Gentlemen Pensioners—tall, handsome men who escorted her on state occasions that entailed contact with the public.

The queen and members of her court at a woodland picnic after a morning's hunt. Although beer and wine were poured freely on such occasions, Elizabeth drank very little alcohol and always liked to dilute her wine with water.

Christopher Hatton (1540-1591), nicknamed "the dancing chancellor" because of his graceful performance at court balls, served as Elizabeth's lord chancellor from 1587 until his death. A skilled diplomat of relatively liberal views, Hatton had a restraining influence on the more extremist members of Queen Elizabeth's court.

court by their parents in order to attract husbands, were guarded possessively by the queen. As monarch Elizabeth insisted on her right to approve marriages in order to keep the nobility under her control. Secret marriages made her furious and resulted in instant loss of favour, if not imprisonment.

The court was the hub of power, the place to go if you were a young gentleman seeking advancement and fortune. In 16th-century England, as in most of Europe, courtiers were no longer from the old noble families but were young men looking for favour and patronage from the queen or important lords like Leicester. Family background was not nearly as important as style and appearance. Courtiers were like actors, concerned with *looking* like gentlemen. A successful courtier also had to be incredibly well-rounded, able to dance, sing, play music, play tennis, hunt, joust or "tilt", speak a few languages, understand the arts—and do all this as if there were nothing to it. Men eagerly read Castiglione's *The Book of the Courtier* to learn all the details.

Since the queen liked and singled out well-dressed men, her courtiers became obsessed with their dress, eager to keep up with the latest fashions. They wore pearls in their ears, and dyed and braided their beards. For a long while Italian styles were very popular. Men often *wore* their fortunes, and the cost of staying could be so overwhelming that many men left the court in serious debt.

Like a film star, Elizabeth loved to be complimented. Though no longer a youthful beauty, she was still a magnetic older woman. She encouraged flirtation as a way of attracting attention and continued to charm men to do what she wanted.

And Leicester was not Elizabeth's only favourite. Christopher Hatton, a young lawyer, first attracted Elizabeth while on the dance floor and caused enough of a stir to make Leicester jealous. Nonetheless, Elizabeth gave Hatton a place in her household. He gradually worked his way up, earning the queen's trust and eventually becoming lord chancellor. A devoted courtier to the end, he never married.

**Italian diplomat and author Baldassare Castiglione (1478–1529) wrote *The Courtier* in 1528. A dialogue on ideal courtly life, it was widely studied by England's nobles after its publication there in 1561.**

# 8

# The Court in Progress

When the court's current residence became too filthy, when even the perfumes and abundant flowers were no longer able to hide the smell, it was time to move. In Elizabethan times, sanitation, especially for such a huge group of people, was a problem. In addition to the garbage, sewage, and the resulting stench, there was the risk of contracting fatal diseases such as smallpox and the plague. The whole enormous court packed its bags, including the queen's bed, which went wherever she did, and prepared to take up residence at another of the royal palaces.

The queen spent her winters in Whitehall Palace in London, where along the Strand, parallel to the Thames, stood the great houses of her peers. Late summer was the time of her royal progresses or tours into the surrounding counties. This was as far as Elizabeth ever travelled. Curiously, she never travelled outside England, nor even far from her palaces. Perhaps, she did not want to leave her seat of power in the hands of others.

A courtier makes a formal bow to his queen. Although 16th-century court etiquette was complex and highly structured, court officials and guests frequently displayed coarse manners. The queen herself sometimes slapped her maids and often swore, a habit that amused her retainers and disgusted the clergy.

The earl of Leicester, master of Kenilworth Castle, provided Elizabeth with the most spectacular entertainments of her reign.

As Elizabeth passed by, the countryfolk would stare at their queen, whom they would probably see only once in their lives. "Thank you my good people," was Elizabeth's customary reply to their cheers. In her gilded coach, she must have looked to them like a fairy queen or a goddess from a dream. The English were beginning to get used to their strange, unmarried queen. After all, she had reigned for nearly 15 turbulent years, fighting off and surviving all the plots against her. And so her strangeness became associated with the aura of good fortune which seemed to surround her.

On these tours the royal procession stretched for miles, winding along the narrow country roads

In 1591 Lord Anthony Montague built an artificial crescent-shaped lake in which he staged an elaborate water pageant for the queen's amusement. Elizabeth's hosts strove to outdo one another in devising gorgeous, imaginative entertainment for her visits.

which were covered with deep, muddy ruts. The travelling court moved at an extremely slow pace. There had to be stops for lunch and for dinner, and at the end of each stretch there would have to be a house where the queen could rest overnight. To provide the supplies to feed the court, the local people were practically stripped bare.

The queen's progresses were generally disliked by her courtiers for they upset the court pecking order. Men would fight about the sleeping arrangements. Beds were occupied in shifts, and many of the court party were stuck in outbuildings or tents. It was next to impossible to do business *en route*. And Elizabeth drove everyone crazy with her habit of

**Flags snapping from its battlements and stirring music echoing through its courtyards, Kenilworth Castle receives Elizabeth and her huge entourage. It sometimes took 400 carts and 2,400 horses to transport the royal procession.**

changing her travel plans at the very last minute.

Her main destinations were the sumptuous houses of her nobles. Although during her reign Elizabeth did little building herself, magnificant mansions were built for her entertainment in the 1560s and 1570s. Entertaining the queen was certainly a tremendous honour, but it was also a terrible expense. Her hosts eagerly wanted her to come, but not to stay *too* long.

Perhaps Elizabeth's favourite place to visit was Cecil's country house. Theobalds, with its multi-coloured bricks and spectacular chimneys. There, water could be piped to the summerhouse and into lead cisterns used for swimming. On the ceiling in the queen's chamber was a clock with stars that moved, and along the walls stood artificial oak trees which looked so real that birds flew in through the windows to sit in the branches.

In 1575 the queen spent three weeks as Leicester's guest at Kenilworth Castle. When she arrived, she was welcomed with a trumpet fanfare from giant pasteboard figures meant to be heralds of the mythical King Arthur. The Lady of the Lake glided by on a floating island in the moat and fantastically costumed characters greeted the queen in verse. In the garden, a fountain squirted people unexpectedly. Delighted, Elizabeth hunted, watched country entertainments and bear baiting—then considered a sport—and admired brilliant displays of fireworks.

In November it was time to return to London and Whitehall. Londoners gathered to see the queen's procession to the chapel or waited in line to watch various court sports. The crowds lined the tiltyard stands to view the tournament celebrating the anniversary of Elizabeth's accession. For entertainment, young courtiers engaged in athletic competition. Across the country, people lit Accession Day bonfires and toasted to their queen. Even if Elizabeth had been excommunicated, she was still their beloved symbol of English and Protestant good fortune.

**Surrounded by richly attired attendants, Elizabeth makes a royal entry to Kenilworth Castle, where she was entertained by her friend Leicester in 1575. The queen encouraged her ministers to build luxurious houses that could easily accommodate her entire court.**

# 9

# A French Match

Strangely enough, in 1579 it seemed that Elizabeth might actually get married. At 45, she was acting as though she might be in love.

In the early 1570s Elizabeth had renewed her marriage negotiations with the French royal family, in the friendly atmosphere created by the treaties signed by the two countries in 1559 and 1572. England finally had a European ally. Religion was proving a stumbling block to marriage, however. Elizabeth and her councillors refused to let her potential husband-to-be, the duke of Anjou, next in line to the French throne, practise his Catholicism in England.

Then, in 1572, came news of St Bartholomew's Day massacre. The Catholic butchery of Protestants spread from Paris throughout France, leaving 50,000 dead. This was just one horrendous episode in the waves of religious violence that swept Europe in the 16th century as Protestants and Catholics tried to destroy each other's beliefs by destroying each other. Although appalled, Elizabeth was too practical to cancel the all-important treaty; but she did call off the marriage talks.

By the late 1570s, Elizabeth was extremely concerned about the situation in the Netherlands, where the Dutch states, present-day Holland and Belgium, were fighting for independence from their

Followers of Gaspard de Coligny (1519–1572), the Huguenot leader who tried to persuade the French king, Charles IX, (1550–1574), to drive Spanish from the Netherlands, are murdered in Paris during the notorious St Bartholomew's Day massacre.

Elizabeth receives representatives from the Netherlands in 1576. Eager to keep the French and Spanish out of the Netherlands, Elizabeth provided financial and military assistance to the beleaguered Dutch.

**Sir Philip Sidney (1555-1586), Leicester's nephew, was a poet, diplomat, and soldier. His letter advising Elizabeth not to marry the duke of Alençon infuriated her; even when he died a hero following a battle against the Spanish in the Netherlands, she refused to attend his funeral.**

Spanish overlords. The French were on the verge of involvement. The duke of Alençon, younger brother of Anjou, who had been making trouble for himself in France, now offered to lead an army with the Dutch to fight against the Spanish. "The Defender of Belgic liberty against the Spanish Tyrant", the Dutch called him.

Elizabeth did not want the Netherlands under French domination any more than she wanted them subject to Spain. In fact, French domination might prove a worse threat to English safety. The best way to control Alençon's activities, she decided, was not to oppose him and become openly involved in war, but to marry him, even if he was 20 years her junior.

In 1579 Alençon's special envoy, Jean de Simier, arrived in England to woo Elizabeth for the duke. The queen warmed to his gallantry and took part in his flirtatious games, letting him steal love tokens for his master and even raid her bedchamber to capture a nightcap. Elizabeth, who had nicknames for all her closest friends and favourites, called Simier "her monkey". She seemed to be enjoying herself so much that Leicester began spreading the rumour that Simier was giving the queen love potions. In public Leicester was supposed to be supporting the French match.

Simier got his revenge on Leicester, however. He had found out about the earl's recent secret marriage. Leicester had had mistresses before, but as he grew older his desire for a legitimate son who would carry on his line became increasingly strong. When Simier revealed the news to Elizabeth, she was furious and hurt, and felt that Leicester had betrayed her at a deeply personal level. Not only had he married, and done so behind her back, but her place had been usurped by a younger court beauty. In anger Elizabeth held him under house arrest, then released him and banished him from court.

Before Elizabeth would make any commitment about her marriage to the French Alençon, she insisted on seeing her potential bridegroom in person. She did not want to be surprised when it was too late, and the reports of Alençon's appearance were not the most encouraging: he was under five feet tall, with a large and bulbous nose, and a face badly scarred and pitted by smallpox.

In the past Elizabeth's insistence on seeing her suitors in person had proved to be a major stumbling block. Most suitors had been insulted by the idea of having to be inspected by a woman. Alençon could journey to her incognito, Elizabeth urged; no one need know about his visit. And to her surprise Alençon agreed.

But of course people knew. After all, Alençon was the first of Elizabeth's suitors ever to pay such a visit. But officially it was a secret and no one was

Queen Catherine de Médici (1519–1589), mother of France's Charles IX, surveys victims of the St Bartholomew's day massacre in Paris. Catherine's violent hatred of the Huguenots, who, she said, wanted to destroy France, led to the orgy of killing that swept the nation in 1572.

William I (1533–1584), also known as the Prince of Orange and William the Silent, led the Protestant Dutch against their Spanish invaders. An ally of Elizabeth, he was hated by Philip of Spain, who had him assassinated in 1584.

supposed to talk about it—at least not in front of the queen. Moreover, the official secrecy meant that Elizabeth and Alençon were free to meet in private. The queen could conduct her courtship as she wanted, without interference from the men in her government.

Alençon did not look as horrible as she had feared. In spite of their differences in age and height, which did make them a very odd couple, the two got on well from the start, with the help of the queen's fluent, graceful French. Elizabeth called Alençon her frog, and to commemorate his nickname, Alençon gave her a brooch of a gold frog sitting on a gold flower, with his face painted on the frog's back. They both enjoyed the playful rituals of courtship and she let herself be captivated, perhaps partly to distract herself from Leicester's betrayal and to get back at him.

When Alençon left after 12 days, Elizabeth was wearing a diamond ring that he had given her, as well as the brooch which shone on her gown. She "would not prevent his being her husband", she said enigmatically.

Would she or wouldn't she? It seemed as if she were serious. And her doctors assured all concerned that she was still capable of bearing an heir. When Elizabeth turned to her council, expecting them to tell her to marry as they had been doing for the past 20 years, they told her what she had always said to *them:* it was up to her. They thought the French were demanding too much in the marriage agreement. Ironically, now that Elizabeth was closer than she had ever been to marrying, she could not get the support she desired.

There was opposition not only in the council but at court. Young Philip Sidney, the poet courtier and ardent Protestant, wrote the queen a letter arguing against the marriage, and in doing so was banished from court as a result. The loudest public opposition took the form of angry sermons and pamphlets by Puritans such as the uncompromising John Stubbs. In his *The Discovery of a Gaping Gulf whereunto England is like to be swallowed by another French marriage if the Lord forbid not the bans by letting her Majesty see the sin and punishment Thereof*, Stubbs claimed that the queen was too old to think of marriage or produce a living child. In addition, he stated that the duke was "the old serpent himself in the form of a man come a second time to seduce the English Eve and to ruin the English paradise".

The queen had always objected to the Puritans who took the Bible, and *their* reading of it, as their only authority. Elizabeth wanted to hang Stubbs and his printer for their audacity. Instead they had their right hands cut off—a cruel enough punishment. Stubbs waved his hat with his left hand, cried "God save the Queen", and fainted.

In 1581, when King Philip of Spain took over the throne of Portugal, he became the ruler of a larger and wealthier kingdom than any European monarch before him. His domains not only spread through Europe but also stretched as far as the Spanish and Portuguese territories in the New World.

However, England too was beginning to explore the New World, and in 1581, after a three-year voyage, Francis Drake returned as a hero, his ships heavy with treasure pirated from the Spanish. Not only was he the first Englishman to sail around the world but he had proven that the Spanish were not sole masters of the waves. As a reward he was knighted by the queen.

Still, Elizabeth needed a strong alliance with the French. There was a real fear that the fanatical Philip would turn his great power against the English adventures and their heretical queen. And Alençon was getting impatient. He did not like being left unanswered, even by the queen of England.

When Alençon returned for a second visit, Elizabeth had to make up her mind. In front of both the French ambassador and Leicester she announced she would marry. She kissed him and gave him the ring from her finger as a pledge. With that, everyone in England and across Europe, including Alençon, assumed that they were married. According to traditional custom, a pledge of marriage was as good as marriage itself.

> *Sceptical and tolerant in an age of growing fanaticism, all English in feeling but pan-European in education, she was born and bred to reestablish the Church [of England], and to evade religious war by a learned compromise between Catholic and Protestant that would leave Crown and [people] masters in their own island.*
> —GEORGE MACAULAY TREVELYAN
> English historian

Philip II of Spain, widower of Elizabeth's half-sister Mary and a one-time suitor for her own hand, eventually became the queen's enemy. His mighty navy was decimated by Elizabeth's depredations against his New World treasure ships.

But Elizabeth vacillated. She decided that finally she could not marry him. Her council and people were against it. And his Catholicism posed a problem. Alençon was also revealing himself to be too eager to drain the English treasury in order to support his army in the Netherlands. Elizabeth bought him off and sent him on his way, the romance over. Thirty months later he was dead. The queen and her court went into mourning, Elizabeth perhaps as much in sorrow for her last possibility of marriage and companionship as for the little French duke.

Guarded by a sword-bearing angel, Queen Elizabeth commands a fleet of ships in a 1577 woodcut that celebrates England's burgeoning naval power.

Sir Francis Drake (1540—1596), the first Englishman to circumnavigate the globe, is knighted by the queen. Although Elizabeth never publicly admitted to financing Drake's expeditions, she made no secret of her delight with the man who "singed the king of Spain's beard" with his attacks on Philip's navy.

# 10

# The Enterprise of England

> *So long as that devilish woman [Mary, Queen of Scots] lives neither her Majesty must make account to continue in quiet possession of her crown, nor her faithful servants assure themselves of safety of their lives.*
> —SIR FRANCIS WALSINGHAM
> Elizabeth I's secretary of state

By the 1580s Catholicism in England was stronger than ever. An increasing number of people were becoming recusants—outwardly refusing to conform to the queen's church and attend church services. Laws against Catholics were toughened, but executing them as traitors only produced martyrs. In fact, priests in training were being schooled to face martyrdom in England.

There grew a real fear that the queen might be assassinated. Uncertainty and dismay filled the country. Even the pope gave his approval to Elizabeth's assassination, saying that the person who did so would not be committing a sin, but instead would be doing God a service. Of course this was great encouragement, and threats were made against her life.

Mary Stuart, still held in captivity after all these years, continued to inspire the Catholic cause in England. Although Elizabeth recognized the threat that Mary presented to her own life as well as to England's political stability, she refused to have her executed. However, Elizabeth would feel unsafe as long as Mary remained alive, as Cecil often told her. Convinced that the queen of Scots' death was

Sir Francis Walsingham (1532–1590), who briefly lost favour with Elizabeth after Mary Stuart's execution, was soon back in her good graces, since the queen depended on his efficiency and intelligence.

Elizabeth liked portraits that emphasized her graceful, slender hands; this particular painting is called "The Ermine Portrait" because it includes one of the animals whose fur was used for royal robes.

An illustration from *The Book of Christian Prayers* shows Elizabeth kneeling in worship. Also known as *Queen Elizabeth's Prayer Book*, it was called "worthy to be read with an earneste minde of all Christians in these dangerous and troublesom daies".

necessary, he was determined to see her removed. Both the council and the people also wanted her dead.

In 1586 Francis Walsingham, the head of Elizabeth's secret service, laid a trap for Mary. Walsingham, a mixture of many characteristics, was a master at uncovering plots and cracking codes, a sophisticated diplomat, and an ardent Puritan set on defeating the Catholic enemy. Discovering a new conspiracy that involved the Scottish queen, he had one of his own men show the conspirators how they could exchange news with the imprisoned Mary. Letters were hidden in watertight containers inside the beer kegs delivered to the castle where she was held. Then, operating with the queen's knowledge, the wily Walsingham intercepted all their correspondence.

In writing, Mary had agreed to the murder of Elizabeth. With this evidence in hand, she was tried by a commission in October 1586, found guilty of treason, and condemned to be executed. Yet even though she now had little choice, Elizabeth could still not bring herself to put Mary to death. How could she mercilessly spill the blood of a woman who was her cousin and a queen? She feared, too, that Mary's execution would anger the French and the Scots, while spurring the Spanish to invade at last.

Before Parliament, assembled primarily to endorse the verdict and see the execution order carried through, the queen apologized for her prolonged indecision and resolved nothing: "Pray you accept my thankfulness, excuse my doubtfulness, and take in good part my answer answerless."

Elizabeth was in agony, perhaps more alone than she had ever been in her life. This was the difficult and painful side of being a queen and wielding the sovereign power which she prized so much. Elizabeth saw herself as having no power above her but God, and she considered herself deeply accountable to God for her actions. She felt that all responsibility for Mary's death would fall on her shoulders, and this was one responsibility she did not want. Yet there was no way to avoid it.

Elizabeth addresses a session of Parliament, convened to ratify the death sentence of Mary, Queen of Scots. "You have laid a hard hand upon me," Elizabeth told the assembled members, "that I must give directions for her death."

By killing another queen she would be destroying her own future. In the eyes of the world she would be seen as a tyrant. "What will they now say," she asked, "when it shall be spread that for the safety of her life, a maiden queen could be content to spill the blood even of her own kinswoman?"

On February 1, 1587, after wavering for five months, Elizabeth called for Mary's death warrant and signed it. When word was sent to Cecil, he quickly rallied the council, fearing that the queen would change her mind. Together the councillors swore an oath to see the execution carried through without further consultation with the queen.

On February 8 Mary went to her death in the hall of

Elizabeth signs Mary's death warrant in 1587. She had postponed the act for months, hoping to find some way of sparing her cousin, but when she learned of yet another Catholic plot to free the imprisoned Scottish monarch, Elizabeth finally approved the fatal document.

Philip II of Spain plotted for years to depose Elizabeth and replace her with the Catholic Mary Stuart. After Mary's death in 1587, he made plans to invade England at once, unrealistically believing that Britons would welcome the Spanish as liberators.

Fotheringay Castle, where she had been tried and condemned. At 44, stiff from 19 years of imprisonment, her hair white under her auburn wig, she walked to the block clothed in red, the colour of Catholic martyrdom.

When Elizabeth heard the news of Mary's death, she was beside herself. For days she could neither eat nor sleep. She had wanted to be rid of this responsibility, but when at last things were taken out of her hands, she lost control. Desperate and like the tyrant she feared the world would label her, she turned on her councillors. They had acted without her authority, she charged. She banished Cecil and Walsingham, and William Davison, the secretary who had taken charge of the warrant, became the scapegoat for the queen's fury. He was sentenced to imprisonment, his career at court destroyed.

Mary's death did not bring the shock waves that Elizabeth had expected. The French barely murmured. Even Mary's son, King James VI of Scotland, acknowledged its necessity. War with Spain became inevitable, however, and at least gave Elizabeth a new focus for her pent-up energy and distress.

Philip of Spain was provoked not only by Mary's death but also by Elizabeth's open involvement in the Netherlands. After having given the Dutch financial support for some time, in 1585 Elizabeth had at last sent over an army in response to Dutch pleas, with Leicester in command. England was officially at war and would be for the remaining 17 years of Elizabeth's reign.

Elizabeth had a deep distaste for war, which was no longer fought in chivalrous one-to-one combat, but more often with guns and gunpowder. She not only desired peace but was acutely aware of her army's weakness. Though she preferred to act defensively and had no desire for military glory, she feared her commanders' desire for it. As a woman, she had to hand over authority to the men who led her troops, and she was not always sure that she could trust them to follow her cautious orders.

The execution of Mary, Queen of Scots. Although the death of the headstrong and romantic Stuart queen guaranteed an attack on England by the Spanish, it united the English people, who had grown weary of Mary's efforts to topple Elizabeth from the throne.

The Spanish Armada, Philip's invasion fleet, was the most powerful any nation had ever put to sea. Its 130 ships were manned by 8,350 sailors, 2,080 galley slaves, and 19,290 soldiers, and it carried 123,790 cannonballs for its 2,630 guns.

Even Leicester was not rewarded with Elizabeth's trust. Under pressure from the Dutch, he accepted the position of governor of the Dutch states, a position Elizabeth had explicitly told him not to take. And in the only battle that he fought, Philip Sidney, the young courtier and Leicester's cherished nephew, died a gallant but wasteful death.

In Spain, Philip was massing his fleet, preparing for the invasion of England, and the English prepared their fleet hoping to be able to stop him. In 1587 Francis Drake attacked the Spanish harbour of Cadiz, burning Spanish ships along with most of the seasoned wood used for storage barrels, something which would prove to be an even greater disaster.

Philip pushed on relentlessly, even though green wood had to be used for the barrels. There was to be no talk of postponement, even when a storm struck the fleet as it prepared to sail, and the chief commander, the duke of Medina Sidonia, began to express his doubts. Philip remained fanatically convinced that God was on his side, and that it was his divine mission to topple Elizabeth. This was to be a holy war. Before they embarked, the Spanish sailors all said mass, and monks accompanied them on board.

In a great crescent formation, with the tallest ships at the outer edges, the "invincible" Armada set sail. In England, wood had been piled on hills along the coast, ready to be lit at first sight of the enemy. The English army camped at Tilbury, ready to drive back the Spanish should they attempt to land.

A fanfare of trumpets and drums echoed through the camp. Like a mythical Amazon queen mounted on a white horse, Elizabeth rode resolutely through the ranks, in gleaming silver armour and a white velvet dress. She was not about to barricade herself into one of her castles in this time of danger, but would show her country what a queen could be. The soldiers, falling to their knees, would not stop cheering.

*As for gentlemen, they be made good cheap in England. For whosoever studieth the laws of the realm, who studieth in the universities, who professeth liberal sciences and, to be short, who can live idly and without manual labor and will bear the [manner, responsibility, and appearance] of a gentleman, he . . . shall be taken for a gentleman.*
—SIR THOMAS SMITH
English statesman and scholar who served Elizabeth I as secretary of state and occasional ambassador.

A bareheaded Queen Elizabeth makes a dramatic speech to her troops at Tilbury. After assuring them that she had "the heart and stomach of a king", the queen promised that "we shall shortly have a famous victory over these enemies of my God, my kingdom, and of my people."

"I know I have the body of a weak and feeble woman," Elizabeth told them the next day, "But I have the heart and stomach of a king, and of a king of England too, and think foul scorn that Spain, or any prince of Europe should dare to invade the borders of my realm."

Meanwhile, the Spanish were facing one problem after another. They proved unable to meet up with their army in the Netherlands, which, under the command of the duke of Parma, was to embark for England aboard specially constructed barges, using the Armada as an escort. While the Spanish fleet waited, the intrepid commander of the English fleet, Lord Howard of Effingham, convinced his captains and admirals to set fire to some of their own ships and then sent the flaming hulks sailing towards the Armada. In fear, the Spanish scattered.

**The "invincible" Armada waits for its rendezvous with Spanish troops from the Netherlands on July 27, 1588. A day later, the proud Armada was in shambles, decimated by brilliantly manoeuvred English fire ships.**

With the English in pursuit, the Spanish headed north, and kept heading north. Soon water ran out and supplies quickly went rancid in the unseasoned barrels. In frustration, the Armada was forced to sail out around Ireland and finally back to Spain, devastated by storms and disease. Only 67 of 130 ships returned, and these were filled with dying men. Even Medina Sidonia was delirious. Bodies of men and horses washed up day after day along the Irish shore.

Since no one in Europe had heard any news of a defeat, bells rang out in celebration of a Catholic victory. The English waited for the Armada to reappear but gradually realized in amazement that the Spanish would not return. Finally it was declared an English victory.

Thus the defeat of the Armada and the execution of Mary only strengthened Elizabeth's position as the figurehead of Protestantism. She was the one who, in spite of everything, seemed invincible. Ignoring their religious differences, even Pope Sixtus V could not help expressing his admiration for the English queen. "What a valiant woman," he exclaimed. "She braves the two greatest kings (of France and Spain) by land and sea . . . It is a pity that Elizabeth and I cannot marry; our children would have ruled the whole world."

In one of history's greatest maritime engagements, the English fleet, its warships smaller and lighter than those of the Spanish navy, disperses the Armada off the coast of France in 1588.

Pope Sixtus V (1521–1590) spoke admiringly of Elizabeth's courage and will, despite the fact that he had financed Philip's ill-starred expedition against England, which was aimed at destroying English "barbarism" and heresy.

ELIZA, TRIVMPHANS

# 11

# Queen of a Golden Age

A new generation came of age and entered court in the war years, the last two decades of Elizabeth's reign. The older generation that had surrounded Elizabeth since she came to the throne was dying off. Leicester, Elizabeth's companion since youth and the man she might once have wished to marry, died just after the Armada victory celebrations.

The young men were restless and eager for action. Life at court did not seem to satisfy them. The queen was a distant figure—not only was she a woman but one from another generation. Although she was growing older, her face worn and her facial make-up heavier, Elizabeth still demanded flirtatious attention from her courtiers, and business was still to be cloaked in gallantry. Yet these mutual games did not have the same spark of personal attachment as before. At court, as in the country, worship of the queen was becoming practically a cult. She was addressed with a variety of highly ornamental names, such as Astrea and Gloriana, as if she were a godddess.

Two new spheres of action presented themselves

Shown in this contemporary illustration as head of state and defender of the Anglican faith, Elizabeth became an object of almost religious veneration in her own time. She was called "the mother of her country" and said to have "glorious endowments, as well of mind as of body, a prince incomparable."

Elizabeth represents triumphant England in this portrait made after the defeat of the Spanish Armada. Although the war with Spain dragged on until Elizabeth's death, the naval victory at Calais was the conflict's turning point. It also served to pave the way for increased English domination of the seas.

**Sir Walter Raleigh (1552–1618) oversees the planting of Elizabeth's royal banner in the soil of Virginia, the New World colony he named for his patron, England's "Virgin Queen".**

to these impatient young men. They could go off to war, striving for military glory against the Spanish, in the Netherlands, or in Ireland, long a trouble spot for the English who tried to govern it. The Irish, aided by the Spanish, were once again rebelling and threatening to overthrow English rule.

Alternatively, the young men could seek adventure in the New World. Exploration by sea had first been undertaken in search of trade routes to the Orient. There had to be a way by which a ship could gain easier access to the spice-producing countries. Spices, a highly profitable commodity, were considered essential to a fashionably correct diet by wealthy Europeans, whose tastes were becoming increasingly sophisticated. In addition, there developed a second motive for sea expeditions: to harass the Spanish ships and their settlements which were monopolizing New World trade. There was also the promise of captured treasures as Drake had discovered.

Later still, there was another purpose—to claim land for England and found colonies, such as the colony of Virginia, which Walter Raleigh named in honour of Elizabeth, the "Virgin Queen". These sea-faring adventurers were real-life heroes who appealed to people's imaginations. Richard Hakluyt's book, *The Principall Navigations, Voyages and Discoveries of the English Nation,* which appeared in 1589, became a bestseller.

Walter Raleigh rose so quickly at court that he was called "the best hated man in the world". He remained a favourite of the queen for 10 years, until he secretly married in 1592. In Raleigh, Elizabeth found another quick and eager thinker like herself, someone who shared her thirst for knowledge and whose wide-ranging experience and curiosity she admired. After all, this was the man who brought potatoes and tobacco from America and introduced them to England. Through Raleigh, Elizabeth could live adventurously, and yet, when it came to giving him political power, she distrusted his recklessness.

Raleigh drew other intellectuals around him, and first introduced the poet Edmund Spenser to court. Spenser's epic masterpiece, *The Faerie Queene,* stands as a poetic commentary on the religious, political, and social aspects of the period in which it was written. Dedicated to Elizabeth and filled with elaborate praise in her honour, it demonstrates that Elizabeth's lifelong balancing act had paid off handsomely. Spenser was himself an ardent Puritan and not entirely happy with Elizabeth's compromise between Protestantism and Catholicism. And yet *The Faerie Queene* could not have been written in an England other than the one Elizabeth had created. In Elizabeth's England Spenser's ideal "Christian gentleman" could go about his business undisturbed by fear of persecution.

Elizabeth's Church of England required only a show of belief from the people. Men were basically free to *think* as they liked—only when dissenters flaunted their opposition to the new unified political and religious order did the government strike back. Indeed, Elizabeth was a pacifist at heart and hated strife of any kind. During her whole reign she put to death only four heretics, none of whom was a Catholic. The only people she punished consistently, and then only after much soul-searching, were those who threatened the unity of her precious state.

The fact that one of England's greatest cultural periods and Elizabeth's unique and intensely un-European regime came into full flower at the same time was no coincidence. Compared with the Catholic past. Elizabeth's was an age which introduced to her country the seeds of those freedoms which Englishmen now take for granted.

As increasing numbers of people—both men and women—began to read, and the growing number of printing presses made books more readily available, writing became more than just an activity for nobles with endless spare time on their hands. Responding to the same stimulus, education became more concerned with expanding human knowledge than with saving men's souls.

Elizabeth's own education had been nourished within the mainstream of humanism. This was an intellectual movement which emerged in Italy during the 14th and 15th centuries and then went on

Elizabeth smiles appreciatively in this illustration of the popular legend about Walter Raleigh spreading his cloak over a puddle to protect the royal feet. A dashing courtier, explorer, and poet, Raleigh had a long and adventurous life.

An allegorical illustration shows Elizabeth, as patron of letters, receiving the work of an author. Elizabeth valued all the arts for their contribution to society. Believing that an educated ruling class was necessary for effective government, she also put a premium on grammar-school and university education.

to influence the rest of Europe. The movement had evolved independently of Catholic teachings, and viewed the world in human terms. It represented a departure from the medieval way of thinking, which had seen the world exclusively in relation to God. In Elizabethan England, where the church had been subordinated to the state so that religion might never again disturb politics, humanism found a fertile haven. Indeed, the humanist commitment of the advancement of learning received official encouragement. Teachers, authors, poets, and playwrights could raise questions and entertain thoughts for which they might have been burned alive a hundred years earlier.

From the outset of her reign Elizabeth had taken a keen interest in England's educational system. Recognizing that great universities such as Oxford and Cambridge were vital to English culture and intellectual advancement, she paid regular visits to them. She insisted that they reflect the kind of nation she was seeking to build, and often appointed her leading statesmen as university chancellors. Visiting Cambridge University in 1564 she demanded only that the students demonstrate "uniformity . . . in apparel and religion". During such outings she also expected to be treated to displays of intellectual fireworks of the same quality as those of which her own intelligence was capable.

As England's leading patron of the arts, she spent large amounts of money on theatrical productions at court and in the universities. Indeed, many plays received their first performances at court. This meant that by the time a play reached the public the whole company had already rehearsed and staged it in ideal circumstances. The actors might often have had to face a hail of rotten eggs but for the fact that Elizabeth's generosity had allowed them to get it right in civilized surroundings before playing to a crowd of rude and boisterous commoners, or groundlings, as they were called.

Plays were becoming increasingly popular with people at all levels of society, though some looked suspiciously at this new phenomenon. The earl of Leicester had established and financed England's

The Globe theatre, where audiences first saw the great dramas written by William Shakespeare (1564–1616). The immortal playwright also appeared as an actor at The Globe, which burned to the ground in 1613 during the premiere of his *Henry VIII*.

first professional theatre company in 1574. Two years later, however, the Puritan-dominated Common Council of the City of London forbade the staging of plays in the area they controlled. They claimed that plays corrupted the youth, attracted thieves and "masterless men", kept apprentices from work, and, with audiences so closely packed together, were breeding grounds for disease. The queen and her nobles immediately intervened by supporting theatre companies of their own. The manager of Leicester's company took the response to the Puritan challenge one step further and organized the construction of England's first public playhouse, The Theatre, just outside the city limits. Other theatres whose names have become immortal soon followed: The Curtain, The Rose, and The Swan.

In 1598 the sons of James Burbage, the founder of The Theatre, told their landlord what they thought of his proposed rent increase, pulled their playhouse down and used the timber to build the theatre which became the most famous in the history of English drama—The Globe.

The plays staged at these theatres by the new professional companies reflected the intellectual ferment of the times. As Spenser had done with his poetry, so too did great playwrights like William Shakespeare and Christopher Marlowe reveal the essence and preoccupations of the Elizabethan Age. Marlowe's *Doctor Faustus* tells the tale of a scholar who agrees to sell his soul to the Devil in exchange for unlimited knowledge. Faustus thus faces the dilemma which confronted all 16th-century intellectual adventurers. In seeking such knowledge he is attempting to put himself on an equal footing with God. Faustus is the supreme example of the "new man", the kind of man whose passion for truths leads him to question the established order. And it was only because Elizabeth had defended and consolidated her father's break with the Catholic regime that such daring plays as *Doctor Faustus* could be freely performed and debated in England.

Elizabeth had long demanded of her most learned subjects that, no matter *what* they thought, they should think it through *well*. She had no time for fools or for people who used their intellectual talents only in support of bigotry and prejudice. When Thomas Cartwright, a leading Puritan and former divinity professor at Cambridge University, proposed the death penalty for all cases of adultery, blasphemy, and heretical opinion, Elizabeth was deeply offended. Such extremism went against everything she stood for.

Elizabeth's church may indeed have been the "leaden mediocrity" its critics considered it. Her kingdom may have seemed a faceless state compared with the European monarchies. And yet it cannot be denied that learning, literature, and science advanced astonishingly fast during her reign. This was perhaps due to the fact that the calculating and rational Elizabeth had forged a new kind of state, one in which there was no room for religious passion, which some historians consider the most divisive and dangerous of all the passions.

The nature of life at Elizabeth's court towards the

THE FAERIE
QVEENE.

Difpofed into twelue books,
*Fashioning*
XII. Morall vertues.

LONDON
Printed for William Ponfonbie.
1590.
ß

Edmund Spenser's *The Faerie Queene*, a long, allegorical poem dedicated to Elizabeth and containing advice about the proper training of a gentleman, has been greatly admired by students of literature for almost 400 years.

Edmund Spenser (1552–1599), author of *The Faerie Queene*, served as secretary to the queen's old friend Leicester, who died alone and virtually unmourned in 1588. "He is now dead," wrote Spenser, "and all his glories gone / And all his greatness vapourized to naught."

Shakespeare salutes Elizabeth in this unknown painter's picture of a meeting between the two towering 16th-century figures. Little is known of Shakespeare's years in London, and no evidence of his encountering Elizabeth exists, although many scholars believe he was acquainted with one of her greatest favourites, the earl of Essex, and his brilliant circle.

Waiting for the drama to begin, playgoers gather outside the celebrated Globe theatre. Early theatres were usually owned in part by the actors who performed in them; the great Shakespeare held shares in The Globe, where he once played the Ghost in his own *Hamlet*.

end of her reign almosts suggests that money had become the new religion! Money ruled everything. Men bribed their way to attention, fought for what money there was to be made, and struggled to stay out of debt. Desperation lurked in the halls and corridors of the court, and in the country at large. Trade had been badly damaged by war and the people had been hit by high inflation. Elizabeth, too, was short of money, her treasury eaten up by military expenses.

At this time two factions divided the court. One was led by Robert Cecil, who had taken his father's place as Elizabeth's key advisor and shared his father's shrewdness, if not all his scruples. Leicester's stepson, the earl of Essex, led the other faction and, just as Leicester had been, was Elizabeth's dashing young favourite.

Essex, whom Elizabeth called her "wild horse", was intelligent, energetic, had flashy good looks, but at times was infuriating. He had no patience for being ruled by the queen's commands, or for staying at court. Hungry for glory, he would rush off on military exploits without telling her.

When in 1590 Elizabeth sent Essex to Ireland to lead a force against the victorious rebels, he made a truce with the rebel leader instead. His army was weakened by disease and Essex returned to England without Elizabeth's permission. He arrived at the palace early one morning and, without washing or changing his muddied clothes, burst into the queen's chamber to offer his excuses.

Elizabeth realized that Essex could be dangerous, but his swashbuckling exploits overseas had also made him popular, unlike any of her past favourites. Killing him might spark off a revolt. Instead, Elizabeth wounded him indirectly but severely—she cut off his income. Bankrupt and desperate, Essex began to plot a revolt. He and his followers, he reasoned, would raise the people of London to arms, seize the Tower, and finally take over the court. Essex ran through the London streets shouting "For the queen, for the queen! A plot is made for my life!" He was captured and soon thereafter executed for treason.

Throughout the court there was an air of insecurity and a yearning for change—not just for a new government but for a new *kind* of government in

> *What, cannot princes err? Cannot subjects receive wrong? Is an earthly power or authority infinite?... I can never subscribe to these principles.*
> —ROBERT DEVEREUX
> earl of Essex

Doctor Faustus, the central character in the Christopher Marlowe (1564—1593) play, *The Tragical History of Doctor Faustus,* stands in a ring of magic symbols as he conjures up the Devil. Belief in supernatural beings was common in the 16th century, and theatregoers found nothing incredible in the sudden appearance of devils, ghouls, and ghosts.

Playwright and poet William Shakespeare, arguably the greatest writer England—or the world—has ever produced, wrote not for the educated upper classes but for the ordinary people of England. They enjoyed his sometimes bawdy comedies, his dramatic histories, and his deeply moving tragedies.

Mʳ. WILLIAM
SHAKESPEARES
Comedies, Histories, and Tragedies.
Published according to the true Original Copies.
*The Third Impression.*

*LONDON,*
Printed for *Philip Chetwinde,* 1663.

which the monarch had less absolute power. Yet at the same time, the ageing Elizabeth had become a legend in her own day. Her oddity as an unmarried woman, which for so long had been the cause of scandal, became central to the cult of the Virgin Queen. And ironically, this is how the fiery Elizabeth would go down in history.

Elizabeth herself was distressed by the fact that England was still war-torn and unstable. Essex's rebellion had shaken her. Given to fits of anger and depression, she carried an old sword around with her everywhere. She had held the country together through the crisis of almost 44 years, and before her death she would see even the Irish rebels surrender. Under her rule England had become an important European power with a strong fleet and substantial holdings in the New World, and London a huge, international city.

There were two events in particular towards the end of Elizabeth's reign, the consequences of which no one could have foreseen at the time. When Parliament met in 1597, the assembled members had convened from the four corners of a kingdom in dire straits. The peasants were starving in the aftermath of three successive bad harvests. The continuing war with Spain had severely disrupted

Elizabeth, infuriated by the rash, unpredictable, and often disrepectful earl of Essex, gives her young courtier a royal slap. Leicester, Essex's stepfather and predecessor as the queen's favourite, had always treated Elizabeth with all due courtesy, but Essex underestimated the steely pride of the ageing monarch, a miscalculation that cost him his head.

Poet John Donne (1573–1631) was one of the many brilliant writers and artists whose work ornamented the last decades of Elizabeth's reign, sometimes called "England's Golden Age". Still often quoted, Donne's writing included such phrases as "Death be not proud" and "Never send to know for whom the bell tolls".

trade with Europe, and many people thought that England was on the verge of economic ruin. A Poor Law was instituted and the administrations of London and other cities were ordered to take whatever steps were necessary to relieve the widespread social and economic distress.

With this enactment Elizabeth's government had elected to take over the charitable role which had been a function of private agencies ever since Henry VIII's dissolution of England's monasteries. This remarkable piece of legislation marked the beginning of a tradition of state aid to the disadvantaged which has lasted in Britain to this day. The modern British welfare state might not be as comprehensive as it is now but for the fact that its seeds were first sown almost 400 years ago.

The other event with unforeseen implications was Elizabeth's granting of a royal charter, in 1599, to "the Governor and Company of the Merchants of London trading into the East Indies". That same disruption of trade with Europe which had partially contributed to the need for the Poor Law encouraged English merchants to ply their trade further afield. Over the next 200 years the East India Company, as it came to be known, gained an economic stranglehold on the markets of the Indian subcontinent. Not until 1948 did the last British soldiers and administrators leave India, the "jewel in the crown" of the British Empire. The eventual return on the original investment of 72,000 English pounds which established the East India Company in 1599 would have left that handful of merchants speechless if they had been allowed a glimpse into the future.

By demonstrating her love for her people, Elizabeth had won theirs in return. "There is no jewel, be it ever so rich a price, which I set before this jewel: I mean your love," she told her last parliament in 1601, in her moving "golden speech".

"To be a king and wear a crown," she continued, "is a thing more glorious to them that see it, than it is pleasant to them that bear it . . . Though you have had, and may have, many princes more mighty and wise sitting in this seat, yet you never had, nor shall have, any that will be more careful and loving."

She could still greet foreign ambassadors in their own tongues, impressing them with her knowledge of languages. Now almost 70, her face was "fair but wrinkled", as one diplomat described, and the teeth that remained were black and caused her severe pain. She insisted on keeping active, however, even when everyone else, including her doctors, thought she ought to slow down. Once, as the court prepared to move back to London in the middle of a storm, one of her courtiers warned her that she should not ride her horse. The old queen responded by mounting her steed and riding the whole way without stopping.

Dr William Gilbert (1540–1603) later called "the father of electricity", shows Elizabeth an experiment with magnetism. Elizabethan scientists made many important discoveries in such fields as metallurgy, biology, mathematics, and navigation.

Elizabeth made great efforts to appear healthy in the eyes of court and country, knowing that her ability to command respect and obedience depended on her show of personal strength and authority. Nor did she want England's safety threatened should rumours of ill health reach the courts of Europe, especially King James's court in Scotland. Although the succession had never officially been settled, it was quietly assumed, even by the queen, that James, the son of Mary Queen of

James I (1566–1625), son of the ill-fated Mary, Queen of Scots, ruled Scotland for 36 years and ascended the English throne when Elizabeth died in 1603. During his reign, scholars produced the "modern" King James Bible, a revised version of the Scriptures.

Surrounded by grieving courtiers, the dying Queen Elizabeth makes her farewells to a world she helped shape and an England of whose affection she was sure. "Though God has raised me high," she said in a last speech to Parliament, "yet this I count the glory of my crown, that I have reigned with your love."

Scots, would be Elizabeth's successor. Keeping his own interests in mind, Robert Cecil was making ready for a smooth transfer of power.

By 1603 James was waiting just as the young Elizabeth had done a half-century earlier. For Elizabeth was growing weaker. She would sit on a pile of cushions on the floor of her chamber and refuse to move or go to bed. When, in the early hours of March 24, 1603, the 69-year-old queen finally died in her sleep, a messenger leaped onto a waiting horse and sped to Scotland. And the new James I of England began his progress south, ushering in the troubled Stuart dynasty.

At Elizabeth's funeral, over a thousand mourners marched in procession while thousands more filled the London streets. No king or queen before her ever received the nationwide show of grief that England now gave Elizabeth. By the end of her reign, few of her subjects, most of whom did not live past 30, could remember a time without her. She had outlived not only her friends but all her enemies as well.

After her death, the longing for the golden past that Elizabeth came to represent grew stronger. This is hardly surprising, since the two kings who reigned after her made a mockery of monarchy. James I was little concerned with showing himself to his people. Once, when criticized for this failing by one of his ministers, he sarcastically suggested that the most his subjects deserved was a sight of his naked posterior. In the fourth decade after Elizabeth's death James's son, Charles I, would add injury to insult. He made the divine right of kings a justification for tyranny and thus plunged the country into a traumatic civil war. His execution by Oliver Cromwell's Parliamentarian government in 1649 would naturally have horrified Elizabeth. And yet Elizabeth, above all a consummate and perceptive politician, knew both her weaknesses and her strengths, and might well have understood why the execution was inevitable.

While Charles I arrogantly demanded the love of the English people, Elizabeth I had always done her utmost to deserve it.

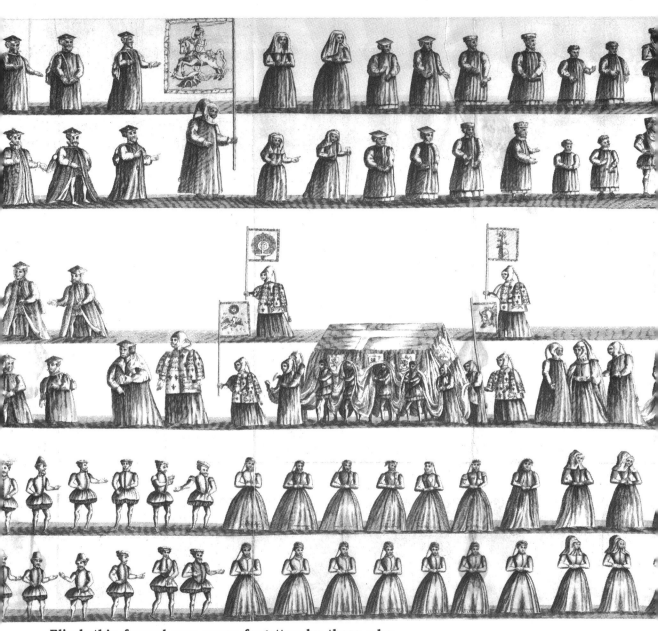

Elizabeth's funeral was never forgotten by those who witnessed it. From the enormous crowd of onlookers there came, according to one observer, "such a general sighing, groaning, and weeping as the like hath not been seen or known in the memory of man."

# Further Reading

Johnson, Paul. *Elizabeth I: A Study in Power and Intellect.* London: Weidenfeld & Nicolson, 1974.

Plowden, Alison. *Elizabeth Regina.* London: Macmillan, 1980.

Rowse, A. L. *Eminent Elizabethans.* London: Macmillan, 1983.

Tillyard, E. M. W. *The Elizabethan World Picture.* London: Penguin, 1986.

Youings, Joyce. *Sixteenth-Century England.* London: Penguin, 1984.

# Chronology

| | |
|---|---|
| Sept. 7, 1533 | Elizabeth Tudor born at Greenwich Palace, near London |
| May 19, 1536 | Anne Boleyn, Elizabeth's mother, executed on the orders of her husband, Henry VIII |
| Jan. 28, 1547 | Henry VIII dies<br>Edward, Elizabeth's half-brother, becomes king |
| July 6, 1553 | Edward dies<br>Mary, Elizabeth's half-sister, becomes queen |
| Jan.-Feb., 1554 | Sir Thomas Wyatt stages rebellion against Mary |
| March 18, 1554 | Elizabeth, suspected of complicity in Wyatt's plot, is confined to the Tower |
| Nov. 17, 1558 | Mary dies.<br>Elizabeth becomes queen of England |
| 1560 | Robert Dudley rises to prominence at court and becomes Elizabeth's favourite |
| 1561 | Mary Stuart returns to Scotland from France |
| July 28, 1565 | Mary Stuart marries Lord Darnley |
| 1568 | Mary Stuart flees to England |
| 1569 | Northern rebellion crushed |
| May 25, 1570 | Elizabeth excommunicated by Pope Pius V |
| April 19, 1572 | France and England sign Treaty of Blois |
| Aug. 24, 1572 | French Catholics slaughter thousands of their Protestant compatriots, temporarily straining relations with England |
| 1582 | Elizabeth decides to end marriage negotiations with the duke of Alençon |
| 1585 | Elizabeth sends army under Leicester to fight the Spanish in the Netherlands |
| 1586 | Mary Stuart tried and found guilty of treason |
| Feb. 7, 1587 | Mary Stuart executed<br>Major conflict with Spain becomes inevitable |
| 1588 | Spanish Armada beaten off by the English navy |
| 1599 | Elizabeth sends her favourite, Robert Devereux, earl of Essex, to crush rebels in Ireland |
| 1601 | Essex's rebellion and execution |
| March 24, 1603 | Elizabeth dies<br>James Stuart, Mary Stuart's son, becomes king |

# Index